"This book is a breath of fresh air for anyone who suffers from obsessive-compulsive disorder (OCD). Instead of just telling you what you should or shouldn't do, the book helps you learn how to relate to yourself with more mindfulness and compassion. Rather than trying to fix or change yourself, the practices actually help you befriend who you are already, allowing you to heal through the power of presence and kindness."

—**Kristin Neff, PhD**, author of *Self-Compassion*

"Wow! This is the most empowering OCD book I have ever read. This mental disorder is a clever and manipulative challenger that requires you to bring your A-game. If you are in it to win it, *Everyday Mindfulness for OCD* is your playbook."

—**Reid Wilson, PhD**, author of *Stopping the Noise in Your Head*

"Too often those with OCD are told 'don't worry,' or 'sit with your anxiety,' as if it were so easy. Hershfield and Nicely are among the top OCD therapists in the field, in terms of both treating it and mastering their own OCD. In this book, their infectious exuberance will provide you with the how-to steps you need to master your OCD and rediscover joy."

—**Jonathan Grayson, PhD**, director at The Grayson LA Treatment Center for Anxiety & OCD

"I was impressed and moved by this book. The authors expertly help the reader to take mindfulness off the meditation cushion and out of the therapy office—and into their lives. Mindfulness, acceptance, and self-compassion can powerfully help us to free ourselves from the stranglehold that anxiety can exert. This is a highly recommended work that I will be using with my clients."

—**Dennis Tirch, PhD**, coauthor of *The ACT Practitioner's Guide to the Science of Compassion*, and founder of The Center for Compassion Focused Therapy

"*Everyday Mindfulness for OCD* can be a lifeline for those with OCD who have found exposure and response prevention (ERP) 'dreadfully hard,' as the authors put it—or worse. By adding mindfulness and self-compassion to the standard therapy, their thoughtful and straightforward strategies and tools—and even games—promise to ease the suffering of countless people with OCD."

—**Sharon Begley**, author of *Can't Just Stop*

"Good books offer pearls of wisdom. Great books string them together in meaningful ways. This book does even more by skillfully weaving such strands into a lifeline that readers can reach for again and again. What a gift Jon and Shala have created for countless OCD sufferers looking for a way back to the joyful side of life!"

—**Jeff Bell**, author of *When in Doubt, Make Belief*

"A must-read for those suffering from OCD and those treating it. Jon and Shala expertly lay out the mindfulness-enhanced approach to exposure therapy for OCD. More than a how-to book, *Everyday Mindfulness for OCD* shows how accepting thoughts without judgment, and with self-compassion, can improve outcomes. We need more books like this."

—**Randy O. Frost, PhD**, Harold Edward and Elsa Siipola Israel Professor of Psychology at Smith College, and coauthor of the *New York Times* bestseller *Stuff: Compulsive Hoarding and the Meaning of Things*

"If you have OCD or help people who do, you need to read this book! Written by two expert therapists who know OCD from the inside out, this book provides an abundance of tools to effectively achieve and maintain mastery over OCD. The authors bring humor, personal experience, and a wealth of wisdom to their writing about how to use mindfulness, self-compassion, and a vast array of creative tools and strategies to stay on top of OCD while continuing to use ERP as a lifelong goal. You'll want to keep this book close by for refreshers on how to creatively and compassionately stay on top of OCD and *joyfully* live your life!"

—**Joan Davidson, PhD**, codirector of the San Francisco Bay Area Center for Cognitive Therapy, and assistant professor in the clinical sciences program at the University of California, Berkeley

"Living with OCD means learning to address intrusive thoughts as they arise, whether while you're chopping vegetables in your own kitchen or navigating a crowded store. With *Everyday Mindfulness for OCD*, Jon and Shala have provided a practical, compassion-filled guide to doing just that. One by one, they clear up misconceptions about meditation (you don't have to clear your mind of all thoughts, thank goodness); mindfulness (it *is* exposure); self-compassion (it's not the same as reassurance); and ERP (it can actually be fun!). They want you to lead a joyful life and, with insight and humor, they show you how that's possible."

—**Alison Dotson**, author of *Being Me with OCD*; president of OCD Twin Cities, an affiliate of the International OCD Foundation; and recipient of the 2016 International OCD Foundation Hero Award

"OCD recovery is about finding the opportunities for growth. Mental health offers the sufferer an opportunity to master their mind. Jon and Shala have written a wonderful book that endorses this mission. Mindfulness and self-compassion are important factors for living joyfully, and this book describes and guides the reader to living joyfully through practical explanations, exercises, and examples. I highly recommend this book for anyone struggling with OCD and looking to regain the vitality in their life!"

—**Stuart Ralph**, curator of *The OCD Stories*

"This eloquent and delightful book combines the most relevant research in the field with the cognitive, behavioral, and mindfulness tools needed to live a full and joyful life with OCD. A truly inspiring read and a bedside table must-have!"

> —**Kimberley Quinlan, LMFT**, licensed marriage and family therapist in the state of California specializing in treating OCD, OCD spectrum disorders, and coexisting eating disorders using mindfulness-based cognitive therapy (MBCT)

"This is a wonderful book! Jon and Shala present the complex intersection of mindfulness, self-compassion, and ERP in plain and simple language that is easy to read and understand. It is not overly clinical nor is it 'preachy.' The authors use helpful illustrations and witty metaphors to clearly explain the acquisition and practical application of certain skill sets to the treatment of OCD. The book's tone is very friendly and positive, and one that offers the reader great empowerment and hope. It is a worthwhile addition to anyone's OCD library, both professional and layperson alike."

> —**Allen Weg, EdD**, licensed psychologist, founder and executive director of Stress and Anxiety Services of New Jersey, and author of *OCD Treatment Through Storytelling*

"This book is a refreshing must-have for people with OCD! Grounded firmly in science and clinical expertise, these authors use easy-to-understand language to build hope and provide practical tools for effectively managing OCD symptoms and living a joyful life!"

> —**Ashley Smith, PhD**, licensed psychologist and anxiety disorder specialist

"This book has just become my absolute favorite for treating clients with OCD and related disorders! It is chock-full of concrete exercises, tools, and even games to engage individuals in treatment. Additionally, it's the first OCD book that thoroughly describes the importance of implementing self-compassion into treatment—an absolute must!"

—**Becky Beaton, PhD**, founder and clinical director of
   The Anxiety & Stress Management Institute in Atlanta,
   GA, and treating psychologist on *Hoarding: Buried Alive*

"*Everyday Mindfulness for OCD* puts on display the passion and understanding Jon Hershfield and Shala Nicely have in their advocacy and treatment for individuals living with OCD. Their writing succeeds in normalizing the debilitating symptoms of OCD, gives practical exercises one can easily practice every day, and offers a light, humorous touch. The plethora of tools and strategies to tackle OCD provided in this book leaves the reader with hope and motivation that there are many ways to attain living in recovery from OCD."

—**Chrissie Hodges**, OCD advocate, peer support specialist,
   OCD therapy coach, treatment consultant, and author of
   Pure OCD

Everyday Mindfulness for OCD

TIPS, TRICKS & SKILLS
FOR LIVING JOYFULLY

JON HERSHFIELD, MFT
SHALA NICELY, LPC

New Harbinger Publications, Inc.

Publisher's Note

This publication is designed to provide accurate and authoritative information in regard to the subject matter covered. It is sold with the understanding that the publisher is not engaged in rendering psychological, financial, legal, or other professional services. If expert assistance or counseling is needed, the services of a competent professional should be sought.

NEW HARBINGER PUBLICATIONS is a registered trademark of New Harbinger Publications, Inc.

Distributed in Canada by Raincoast Books

Cover design by Amy Shoup; Acquired by Wendy Millstine; Edited by Kristi Hein

---

Library of Congress Cataloging-in-Publication Data

Names: Hershfield, Jon, author. | Nicely, Shala, author.
Title: Everyday mindfulness for OCD : tips, tricks, and skills for living joyfully
     / Jon Hershfield, MFT, and Shala Nicely, LPC.
Description: Oakland, CA : New Harbinger Publications, Inc., [2017] |
     Includes bibliographical references.
Identifiers: LCCN 2017016907 (print) | LCCN 2017029228 (ebook) | ISBN 9781626258938
     (PDF e-book) | ISBN 9781626258945 (ePub) | ISBN 9781626258921 (paperback)
Subjects: LCSH: Obsessive-compulsive disorder. | Mind and body. | Cognitive therapy. |
     BISAC: PSYCHOLOGY / Psychopathology / Compulsive Behavior. | BODY, MIND &
     SPIRIT / Meditation.
Classification: LCC RC533 (ebook) | LCC RC533 .H467 2017 (print) | DDC
     616.85/227--dc23
LC record available at https://lccn.loc.gov/2017016907

Printed in the United States of America

23   22   21

10   9   8

To people with OCD at every step of the journey

Contents

Foreword

Obsessive-Compulsive Disorder (OCD) was once considered untreatable. Individuals with OCD could spend years in psychotherapy with minimal or no benefit, and medications available at the time were largely ineffective. Fortunately, the outlook improved dramatically by the end of the 20th century. In addition to a class of drugs called serotonin reuptake inhibitors, a specific form of cognitive behavior therapy known as "exposure and response prevention" (ERP) emerged as a first line treatment for OCD. Receiving a diagnosis of OCD no longer meant a lifetime of hopelessness. With proper therapy, many people could expect to have a significantly better life.

For those of us in a profession dedicated to helping people with OCD, the challenges we face today are quite different. We now know how to help many OCD sufferers, but also recognize the limitations of existing treatments. As a consequence, our efforts to advance the field are focused on discovering alternative or complementary interventions that work more rapidly, reduce symptoms more completely, or have fewer adverse effects than current treatments.

One hope for improving outcomes is to identify factors that might complicate or interfere with treatments like ERP and to develop strategies to modify those factors. *Everyday Mindfulness for OCD* is a fine example of this approach. In this book, Jon Hershfield and Shala Nicely attempt to enhance ERP by addressing behavioral obstacles like trying to control unwanted thoughts, toxic self-criticism, and seclusion from joyful experiences.

To combat counterproductive behavior, the authors offer strategies that can guide your effort to overcome OCD. As the title suggests, much of the book is focused on mindfulness. Being mindful teaches you how to reverse futile attempts to eliminate unpleasant thoughts, and how to accept and move past the things you cannot control. To help you abandon unforgiving self-criticism, Hershfield and Nicely prescribe exercises designed to promote self-compassion. Enhancing self-compassion includes making a concerted effort to recapture the joy that once occupied your life, not simply reducing the misery associated with OCD.

The fundamental principles of ERP have always included the imperative to stop avoiding anxiety-provoking experiences. From the perspective of cognitive behavior therapy, avoidance is the enemy of recovery and it perpetuates OCD. That means anything that facilitates your ability and willingness to counteract avoidance should enhance your chances of recovery. In this book, you will be encouraged to follow the time-honored principles of ERP, but you will also have the opportunity to learn additional concepts and strategies designed to enhance your ability to be mindful, self-compassionate, and, ultimately, to stop avoiding important aspects of your life. I hope you will embrace this opportunity. Good luck!

    —C. Alec Pollard, Ph.D.
        Director, Center for OCD & Anxiety-Related Disorders
        Saint Louis Behavioral Medicine Institute
        Professor Emeritus of Family & Community Medicine
        Saint Louis University

Introduction

This book is about developing mastery over obsessive-compulsive disorder (OCD) in the long term. It's about not just living *despite* OCD, but living *joyfully* with the disorder. In the pages ahead, our aim is to explore how the use of mindfulness and self-compassion can contribute to this project of living joyfully with OCD, both by offering new tools and perspectives and by enhancing traditionally effective ones.

OCD is a psychiatric condition characterized by the presence of obsessions and compulsions. Obsessions are unwanted thoughts that are perceived as intrusive and repetitive. Compulsions are physical or mental behaviors aimed at decreasing the discomfort associated with obsessions. The presence of obsessions and compulsions becomes a clinical issue when there is a related impairment of functioning or quality of life (American Psychiatric Association 2013).

OCD can manifest in a variety of ways. It is not possible to list every kind of obsession and compulsion here, but more typical themes include:

- Contamination: Excessive concern with germs, bodily fluids, chemicals, and the like

- Checking: Excessive concern with being responsible for making sure things are as they are "supposed" to be; for example, doors are closed and locked, appliances are powered off, items are where they belong, and so on

- Just right: Excessive concern with symmetry or exactness

- Harm: Excessive fear of committing acts of violence toward oneself or others

- Sexual themes: excessive intrusive thoughts about sexual orientation or sexual appropriateness

- Relationship: excessive concern with whether a relationship is "right"

- Hyperwareness/Sensorimotor: Excessive concern with awareness of involuntary processes such as blinking or swallowing

As obsessions are unwanted, intrusive thoughts, you become uncomfortable when you become aware of them. It bothers you that the thought is there, in part because it just doesn't line up with what makes sense for you and your identity. You may also associate the thought (specifically, the words or images that make up the content of the thought) with things that are upsetting or disgusting. Naturally, like the secret "normie" that you are, you don't like feeling bad. So you set out to get some certainty that your obsessive thought is harmless or inaccurate, or at least that it will go away. Once you have achieved this in your mind, you give yourself permission to move on, or to return to what you were doing before the obsession so rudely intruded. This behavior is a compulsion.

The problem with compulsions is that they work—at least a little bit, some of the time. Compulsions usually provide some modicum of relief from the pain of your obsessions. This triggers a fascinating process called *negative reinforcement*. By removing pain, compulsions trigger the brain to calculate that the compulsion is tied to the obsession in a manner that should be repeated. This not only increases the urge to respond to obsessions with compulsions, but also increases your sensitivity to the obsession in the first place. When it makes itself known, it does so along with the message that it requires a compulsive response because it feels like a really big deal.

It's like you're getting slapped in the face for no discernible reason, then you stand on one foot and the slapping stops, so your brain thinks you should stand on one foot whenever you see a hand approaching your face. The more compulsions you do, the more you reinforce the cycle. The obsession grows stronger, the drive to do compulsions grows along with it, and around and around you go. To beat an obsession, you need to starve it out, which means you need to target and eliminate compulsions.

Cognitive behavioral therapy (CBT) is a form of psychological treatment that emphasizes challenging distorted ways of thinking about our experiences (cognitive) and making changes in behavior that enable you to face your fears (behavioral). A specific form of CBT called *exposure and response prevention* (ERP) works by having you gradually put yourself in the presence of the thoughts, feelings, or experiences that cause you discomfort (exposure) while resisting attempts to use physical or mental compulsions to neutralize or avoid the discomfort (response prevention). Relatively recent research has shown that exposure therapy violates your brain's expectations about the meaning of the OCD trigger, and in doing so, helps your brain develop inhibitory learning. Over time, the inhibitory learning suppresses the previous fear-based learning about the OCD trigger (Craske et al. 2008). Further, the more you do ERP, the less anxiety you may experience in the face of the same triggers—a process called *habituation*.

One form of CBT, known as acceptance and commitment therapy (ACT), emphasizes openness to thoughts and feelings and a focus on the pursuit of clear values. Different people may respond differently to traditional CBT and ERP approaches, ACT approaches, or some combination. Traditional talk therapies or therapies that focus primarily on relaxation are less likely to be effective for OCD.

Mindfulness is the ability to observe your experiences without judgment. Self-compassion is the ability to relate to yourself with the desire to reduce your own suffering. Together, they form a skill set that can aid you in making healthy decisions about your OCD and maintaining a stable attitude about the disorder every day, even as it waxes and wanes throughout your lifetime.

About the Authors

Jon Hershfield

One of my earliest memories is an OCD memory. I was about five years old, and it began with me telling my mother about a dream I had had the night before. I began to wonder why I was doing this and whether or not there was something wrong about having the dream or wrong about sharing it. I shrugged it off.

Later that day, playing with my friend, I remember sitting on the floor under a table, a bowl of carrots between us, pretending to be rabbits. I felt a tug in my throat, like my stomach was trying to eat my Adam's apple. Something was wrong. I had done something wrong. I was wrong, somehow. I started to cry. I started to scream. My friend became upset, his mom became upset, everyone was very upset. My friend's mom asked, "What's wrong? What is it?" I forced the words through tears: "I—don't—know!!!!!" I consider this my first experience with OCD.

Striving to overcome my lifelong OCD challenges has been a series of ups and downs, with a variety of big wins and dark times throughout the years. It is a story that consistently gets better, but it remains an ongoing journey. *Everyday Mindfulness for OCD* is written as much for me as it is for you, the reader. It is a reminder that developing mastery over many years is a privilege. It is an exploration of tools, techniques, interventions, and mostly attitudes that make long-term management of this disorder a worthwhile endeavor, and I hope it serves as a helpful companion on your path.

Shala Nicely

I've had OCD all my life, but I went for years not knowing that the horrific thoughts that plagued me and the strange little rituals in which I participated had a name. Even after I was diagnosed, I spent many more years in and out of therapy before stumbling upon the evidence-based treatment for OCD, exposure and response prevention therapy (ERP), during the 2010 International OCD Foundation conference.

Since learning about this life-changing treatment, I have done two things: I went back to school to get a master's degree in counseling so I could help others with OCD get the right treatment faster than I did, and I have made ERP an integral part of my life. I know from personal experience how dreadfully hard ERP can be, so I've spent the last several years trying to figure out ways to make it more palatable for my therapy clients and for myself. What I've found is that learning to not just *do* ERP, but to *have fun with it*, doesn't just make your life good—it can make it great, even with OCD quietly tagging along in the background.

I think it's safe to say that in the years since that fateful conference I've had enough experience with life with OCD and with ERP to say with conviction that even if the cards we are dealt have OCD written all over them, we can still hold a winning hand.

About This Book

If you are new to the disorder, the tips and tools in this book can still be instrumental in your recovery, but we recommend you start with CBT/ERP treatment from an OCD specialist or, if that is not an option, self-treatment using one of the self-help resources available (see https://iocdf.org/books/ for a comprehensive list). After that, you may find this book to be most useful as a collateral resource. Medication may also play an important role in your recovery. Though not every person with OCD takes medication, many find it an important factor in treatment when it helps to reduce the intensity of intrusive thoughts and increases the ability to resist compulsions. To assess whether medication could play a role in your treatment, we recommend a comprehensive evaluation from a psychiatrist.

This book is like a user's manual for long-term management of OCD, divided into three parts: mindfulness and self-compassion, daily tools and games to promote joyful living, and different aspects of successful long-term mastery of the disorder. Part 1 will discuss two foundational elements for promoting mastery of your OCD: mindfulness and self-compassion. The shift in perspective that mindfulness affords us can be used to enhance what works in navigating OCD and to reduce what doesn't. In chapter 1 we will review basic mindfulness concepts as they apply to OCD and the role of meditation as a tool for increasing mindfulness skills. In chapter 2 we will explore the essential component of self-compassion. You are the person living with this disorder, and you are the person who is going to master it. So learning to love and support yourself with compassion is a key element in learning to stay on top of your OCD. These two concepts, mindfulness and self-compassion, will be woven into each of the following parts of the book. We therefore recommend that you complete reading part 1 before getting into the tips and tools in part 2.

Part 2 is composed of tools, tips, and games that you can incorporate into your daily experience of OCD. In chapter 3 we describe a variety of meditation and self-compassion exercises, as well as tips for thinking more mindfully about your unwanted thoughts. Chapter 4 includes a variety of ERP exercises (or "games") for tackling the OCD head on. Not every one will click for you, but you can try them out and decide which ones are keepers.

What sets OCD apart from other so-called "chronic" conditions is that you can expect to get better and better as time goes on if you use the right tools and do your maintenance work. One way to think about long-term recovery from OCD is in the form of a curve:

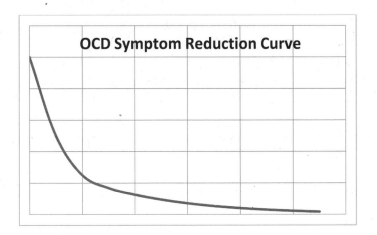

Once you start to make headway in treatment, improvement can be pretty dramatic. Your symptoms may persist for some time, but once you get some momentum going, your symptoms may diminish rather quickly (think weeks or months rather than years). But as you get better and better, this progress slows and never really gets down to zero. You indefinitely approach mastery over OCD, but you never arrive at the complete and total absence of the disorder. Part 3 therefore focuses on issues related to this indefinite approach, such as taking ownership of your OCD, addressing lapses and relapses of your symptoms, and understanding OCD in the context of the larger system in which you live. Living with OCD as a long-term project means persisting in developing your mastery over it. If mastering OCD is a new effort for you, we hope this book takes some of the mystique out of what lies ahead. If you're an old pro, we hope this book offers you some new tools for your toolbox and maybe even adds a kick to your step.

PART ONE

Mindfulness and Self-Compassion for OCD

In this first part of the book, we will explore two key concepts: mindfulness and self-compassion. Understanding some of the basic concepts associated with mindfulness, such as the ability to observe thoughts without judgment, can be a useful tool in navigating OCD issues without falling for compulsive traps. By learning to be compassionate toward yourself along the way, you can gain important insights and motivation. Together, they may make the difference between just getting by and boldly getting well.

CHAPTER 1

Mindfulness

In this chapter, we'll discuss mindfulness in the context of having OCD. Don't be ashamed of thinking at this point that mindfulness is that thing that people with OCD can't do, or associating mindfulness with trying really hard to ignore your thoughts and pretend they don't bother you. In the pages ahead, we will explore what mindfulness is and ways you might conceptualize it that reveal it as tailor-made for the obsessive mind. By learning to be a better observer of your mind, you may also become a better master of your OCD.

Why Mindfulness for OCD

When you have OCD, it's easy to get caught up in the minute details of your thoughts. OCD sufferers are people who see, without even trying, the fine print of the human experience. It's not just a curse, though it can be very painful. This fine attention to detail is an asset as well. The OCD sufferer is a *noticer*. You may notice the way your partner's mouth curves into a smile in a slightly crooked way, and that becomes another thing to love. You may notice that the color of the sky shifts from orange to purple at the horizon, but not until it just barely reveals a color for which we have no name. And this becomes another thing to admire. You may notice the bass line to an otherwise mediocre song and find something to really get into. This enhanced attention to detail in the mind lends itself to creativity, humor, and ingenuity. Being able to enjoy the fruits of a *noticer's* mind necessitates being able to shoulder the burdens of that same mind. Noticing that your shoelace may have dragged along the sidewalk by a puddle filled with unknown liquid, that your door may not have made the signature clicking sound it usually does when you lock it, or that nothing but free will stands between you, the kitchen knife, and a violent encounter with someone you love—this kind of noticing is something you need to make space for as well. It comes with the equipment.

If you want to let yourself be carried off by the *positive* things you notice and return safely from that experience, you have to be able to observe when you've been carried off by *negative* experiences and return safely from those as well. Indeed, this is really the main problem with OCD. You get pulled away from the present moment by obsessions, and by the time you realize that this has happened, you are so deep into it that it requires great effort to disengage. These efforts to disengage from unwanted thoughts, feelings, and sensations come in the form of judgment, analysis, rationalizations, and neutralizations (in other words, compulsions). But what if there were another way? What if you could (1) increase the speed with which you realize that you've been distracted by your thoughts and (2) return from that distraction without preconditions (that is, without rituals)? That skill is called *mindfulness*.

What Is Mindfulness?

Mindfulness, simply defined, is nonjudgmental awareness of the present moment. To experience the world mindfully is to observe it (both the external and internal) without evaluation, in the here and now, with no expectation or mandate to change it. In other words, it is using your noticing abilities to your advantage by stepping back and watching thoughts, feelings, and sensations as they arise. Mindfulness isn't an intervention. You may hear people say things like, "I was really scared, but then I *used* mindfulness." This fails to capture the true nature of mindfulness. Mindfulness is a way of experiencing the world, not something you *do* to it.

A Mindful Example of OCD

Imagine for a moment that you are driving down the road when, all of a sudden, your OCD suggests that perhaps you weren't paying enough attention at the last intersection and you might have run a red light. And not only that—maybe in running the light you caused a horrific accident and someone is now really hurt or maybe even dead because of you. A non-mindful approach to dealing with that obsession would be to react to the anxiety you are feeling ("I feel anxious, so something must be wrong!"), believe the obsession ("Oh, no! I may have killed someone!"), and start acting as if that obsession were true ("I must turn the car around now so I can go back and check to see if everyone's okay!"). This sequence of non-mindful events, of course, leads to a full-blown OCD episode.

A mindful approach to dealing with this obsession is quite different. Viewing the experience mindfully, you would start by simply noticing that this obsession just popped up in your mind. You see it as just a thought that has arisen. "Hey, look at that, there's my mind again, coming up with one of those thoughts." You become aware that you are feeling anxious, recognizing the telltale body sensations that can accompany your OCD: "I'm feeling my heart race, and my hands are getting sweaty." If you are used to having this come up in your OCD, you might also note that this experience is typical of your OCD: "Looks like I'm having one of those OCD triggers." You then notice an urge to go back and check the road for evidence of your imagined crime. Rather than give in to this compulsion to get certainty about your obsession, you simply notice the presence of that urge: "I'm feeling an urge to go back and check." You then make the decision to allow yourself to be in the presence of that urge (instead of dwelling on whether or not to do compulsions) and then bring your attention back to the present moment. You continue driving down the road toward your destination in the presence of your internal experience (your thoughts and feelings) while also being aware of what's going on in the external world (cars passing you, vehicles entering and leaving the road around you, and so on).

Stepping Back

Mindfulness keeps us from fusing with our thoughts and feelings—even those created by obsessive-compulsive disorder. Being mindful does not mean pushing thoughts away or clearing our minds of obsessions or the urges to do compulsions; rather, it allows us to step back and see them for what they are, and this distance makes it easier for us to stop confusing the perceived intensity of the content of the thoughts with their importance.

Joseph Goldstein, one of the people who originally brought the mindfulness tradition to the United States from the East, shared that sometimes he will play a game where he pretends that all the thoughts he's having are coming from the person next to him (Goldstein and Harris 2016). Take a moment to consider that frame of reference. If you could see the thoughts of the person sitting next to you as they occurred, scrolling by as if on a news stream on the bottom of a TV screen, you would just watch them, mostly without much emotion. You might find some of them interesting, boring, shocking, or entertaining, but overall they wouldn't pack the same emotional punch as those same thoughts coming from your own head—in fact, you might have a hard time staying focused on these thoughts coming from another person's mind because to you they just don't have any meaning. That's why learning mindfulness in the context of OCD is so powerful: it helps you recognize that no thought is inherently more meaningful than any other thought, regardless of its content.

Framing your experience this way is no easy feat in the face of disturbing thoughts, painful feelings, and powerful urges to respond compulsively. And yet, if we can position ourselves as observers, rather than victims, of the mind, we immediately have the upper hand over OCD. To give this more clarity, let's talk about another metaphor for how to conceptualize mindfulness.

Staring at the Computer, Metaphorically

One way of understanding mindfulness is to think of awareness in three parts: the brain, the self, and the mind. The brain is that gelatinous mass in your skull. The self is you.

17

And the mind is the interface with which you and your brain interact. Consider that the brain is somewhat like a computer hard drive. It creates, calculates, and stores data. This data is presented and displayed on a screen, like the computer monitor. This screen can be considered the mind in this metaphor. Though you may often hear about the mind doing this or that, being very active, you might also think of it as simply a stationary display of what is going on in the brain. It may have a lot of information on it, or a little. It may have a beautiful and serene backdrop (your wallpaper) or it may be cluttered with pictures, files, folders, and so on.

You are the *self*, the person who decides how much and what *kind* of attention to pay to the various things displayed on the monitor. You might focus most of your attention on an e-mail in front of you, a little attention to some software update alert off to the side, and almost no attention to the different icons in your toolbar at the bottom. This attention can be shifted at will from one thing to another in different parts of the screen.

Problems occur when we find ourselves positioned too close to the screen. Imagine your nose squished up against a computer monitor, trying to process what's going on. Whatever is directly in front of your eyes will get 100 percent of your attention, and whatever it is will seem severe, distorted by the intensity of its being right in your face. This is what it is like to be mind-*less*. You just can't take it all in from that close. So to be mind-*full* you must have enough distance from your mind (the monitor) to take it all in.

Establishing a Healthy Distance from the Screen

People in general, but people with OCD especially, can find themselves too close to the screen of their mind and overwhelmed by whatever piece of data is being presented at any given time. This is why you may have a thought about being dirty and then immediately *feel* dirty. Or you may have a thought about committing a bad act and immediately *feel* guilty. The notion of thoughts just being thoughts seems ridiculous when the thought is demanding all of your attention and flashing so closely to your eyes. So the trick is to back up and get some distance. From a reasonable distance, we can see all of the little bits of data on the screen and *choose* how much attention to give each thing—a little, a lot, or all of it. *None*, as you may have noticed, is usually not on the table. The farther away from the screen, the easier it is to choose what to focus on. Move back even farther, and we may choose to release a focus on our thoughts altogether. But if we can strive to be more mindful and back up from the screen even just a bit, we can live more mindfully and as joyfully as we choose.

The trick is to become aware of when we have gotten too close to the screen and use this awareness as a cue to back up and give ourselves some distance.

Developing Mindfulness through Practice

To practice mindfulness, at least in the context in which we are using it, is to develop greater skill in being mindful, or to give ourselves distance from our metaphorical screen. One way to conceptualize this is to consider that you have a kind of muscle in your brain that brings you back from your obsessions. It is not literally a muscle, of course, but a muscle in the sense that this part of the brain can be exercised and strengthened to improve its performance. If you are trying to stick with the present moment and your obsession pulls you away, distracting you from that present moment, then in order to be present again you need to somehow pull yourself back. But when the glue that binds you to your obsession is stronger than your drive to come back from it, you get stuck. You end up using compulsions to get back, and compulsions are the fuel for your OCD. However, if you have an internal willingness—a muscle that you have exercised and is thus very strong—it can supersede the OCD and allow you to bring yourself back to the present moment. One way to exercise that muscle in your brain is meditation.

The Exercise of Meditation

In the context of OCD, meditation is an exercise and nothing more—like weightlifting for people in training for an athletic event. It is not a religious rite or a path to self-realization. It is not even a tool for relaxation (though it can sometimes be used that way). Quite simply, meditation is an act of mental fitness or mental hygiene wherein you repeatedly flex and contract your ability to pay attention to the present moment. There is no one perfect way to meditate for OCD, but the vipassana tradition is probably the most appropriate for these purposes. Vipassana comes from an ancient Indian practice; it is a Pali word that can be translated as "insight meditation." In this type of meditation, we gain insight in part by focusing on the body and its sensations, and most commonly, on the breath. In a larger sense, vipassana is a series of philosophical and moral perspectives, but one of the tools used to achieve this perspective is a form of meditation that involves training the mind to become aware of when it is distracted by thoughts or feelings and to remain attentive to the present moment (Goldstein 2013).

In the pages that follow, we've broken down an example meditation into a basic format you can use to enhance your OCD-fighting strengths:

- Finding a suitable place to meditate

- Positioning yourself in the space

- Scanning your body

- Watching your breath

- Ending the meditation

Let's take a look at each of these in turn.

Location, Location, Location: Finding a Suitable Place to Meditate

The most helpful environment for meditating is one where you feel you have privacy and are not going to be disrupted. This may seem like a challenge, but do your best to identify a suitable space. If you have kids or you work or go to school, there are surprisingly few locations where you can just sit and be without something or someone asking for your attention. So you need to make the best of what you have available. Your bedroom or any room where you can feel genuinely alone is a good place. If your car is the only place where you can find this, that is fine—just don't try to meditate while driving, please. Meditating outdoors can be good if you have access to an isolated and peaceful place. In general, just consider whether the space you are choosing is at least limited in its distractions.

*Comfortable But Dignified: Positioning Yourself
in the Space*

The traditional approach to meditation, sitting on a cushion on the floor, is not for everyone; if you can do so comfortably, great. But if not, we recommend sitting in a comfortable chair with good back support, adding a pillow behind your lower back if you need additional support. You can meditate lying down, but this might put you at greater risk of falling asleep.

Start by sitting in a comfortable, but upright position, without straining or slouching; if in a chair, with your feet planted on the floor and your hands resting on your knees or thighs. It can be helpful to get in the mood before doing the work, so start by simply taking a few deep breaths and considering a simple concept: "Here I am…in this space." Remember, the point of the meditation is to develop or strengthen the skill of returning to the present moment, so the more clear you are about the present moment, the better. After a few breaths and taking in your immediate environment, close your eyes and just breathe normally (in and out through your nose). If you tend to get dizzy or nauseous with your eyes closed, you can do this exercise with your eyes open, resting your vision on a space a few feet in front of you.

You may have heard meditation directions like "clear your mind." That's fine *for other people,* especially those who don't have OCD, but if you want to use meditation as an exercise to develop better mastery over the disorder, don't attempt that clear-your-mind stuff. OCD sufferers are busy-minded people, and the aim is to soften this busy-ness, not become empty. When thinking happens, the aim of mindfulness is to be *aware* that you are thinking instead of being lost in thought. The moment you close your eyes, you are likely to be very aware of your thoughts, feelings, and sensations. It will get noisy in there pretty quick. Just allow that to be. This is where you are in *this* moment, so it's still perfectly welcomed in your meditation. Remember, the idea is, "Here I am…in *this* space."

Your meditation is not about calming down or being mentally still. It's actually quite active. So start by noticing all those thoughts and feelings and sensations. Go ahead and comment gently to yourself about how you're feeling in this moment. "Wow, there's a lot going on there" is a perfectly mindful statement. "Ugh, I am terrible at this, what a waste" is not so useful (and not so self-compassionate, which we'll get to later).

Print Yourself: Scanning Your Body

Next, you are going to check in with your body, so to speak, first by focusing on and scanning a few key areas and then by doing a full body scan. To begin, *actively* direct your attention to your feet. For the next minute or so, try to mentally sketch out all the various aspects of your experience that are happening right now. So, considering the soles of your feet, mentally draw the areas of your feet that are in contact with your shoes or the floor. Again, "Here I am in this space, my feet pressing down in this way." Let all of your other thoughts circle you and just keep coming back to this task of creating a mental image of the experience of your feet resting on the floor. There's no right or wrong here, so don't get too caught up in doing this "right." If you start by just thinking about your feet, that's not the main objective, but it's fine. If you can observe the experience of how your feet *feel*, the sensation of each foot resting on the floor, that's getting off on an even better foot. (Admit it—that's a functional pun.)

Next, scale back your attention from your feet and shift it to your buttocks. Yes, this is also a glute exercise! Notice how you are pushing down on the seat, or rather, you are being pulled into the seat by gravity and the seat is pushing back against you. If you notice pressure on one side more than another, good. Just go ahead and notice that experience.

Now switch your attention to your hands. Mentally outline your fingers and sketch in your palms, paying special attention to where your hands are touching or not touching your legs. All of this may seem quite busy, which is fine. If you get distracted, also fine. Just notice when you've become distracted and return to what you were doing. At this moment, you are attending to your hands resting on your lap in this moment in this space.

Next, shift your attention to your face. Check in with whatever is going on there. Can you feel the air on your face? Is it warm or cold? Are there any smells or tastes worth noting? Now to your ears. Imagine, if you can, opening up your ear holes to the space you are in. Instead of the sounds you may encounter (an air vent, distant voices, your own breath, a fan, footsteps, and so on) being *problems*, try to view them as simply elements of the space you are in. Too much noise can be too distracting, of course, and may mean this is not an ideal space for meditating. But some noise can add shape and texture to your environment. If there are too many dynamic sounds distracting you, it's perfectly fine to turn on a fan or white noise machine.

Between sitting and arriving at this point, you may have spent thirty seconds or several minutes. This is entirely up to you.

The final scanning step is the full body scan. A good way to think of scanning the body is that your mind is like an inkjet printer. It goes back and forth, back and forth, again quite actively, printing out line by line what it sees until it has produced a complete picture. Starting at the top of the head and gradually, slowly, and evenly working your way down to your feet, print out a mental picture of your body. This print-out is not just what you think your body *looks* like in this moment, but what it feels like too. It's your *experience* of your body. If at any point you come across a part that's uncomfortable or that raises strong feelings, don't stop printing. Just notice what's going on there and let the printer move on evenly. At the end, you will have checked in with all of your points of contact, your senses, and your body as a whole in this space in this moment of time. You are now ready to begin the *meditating* part of meditation.

Resting Your Attention: Watching the Breath

There are many different ways to practice meditation, but for strengthening your mindful muscles against OCD, we will be focusing on a breathing meditation. For the next segment of the meditation exercise, you will rest your attention on your breath. This means shining a spotlight in your mind on where you feel your breath the most. It could be the whoosh as it enters your nose, or the sensation of your solar plexus rising and falling, or the feeling of your belly inflating and deflating. This is your *anchor*. Home base. For the next few minutes, this is the thing you will keep coming back to: this feeling of breathing in and breathing out.

You *will* have thoughts that disrupt your attention on the breath. This is perfectly fine. All distractions are just that: distractions. The idea is to become aware that you have wandered off, simply acknowledge this, and then return to the breath. This, in and of itself, is being mindful and practicing mindfulness.

It doesn't matter if you catch yourself wandering away from the breath a little or a lot. Your mind is like a puppy that you're training to sit or roll over, and it easily gets lured away by things in its environment (like an enticing smell or a bug it could chase). To bring the puppy back, you have to be gentle, friendly, and patient, and above all, you'll want to just remember that puppies are like this: prone to distraction.

Actually, in the beginning at least, wandering off a lot is a *good* thing. Remember, what you are trying to teach yourself is to notice when you've wandered away from your anchor and to return without precondition. If you never wander off, there's nothing to notice and there's no opportunity to strengthen that coming-back muscle. And again, it is this muscle in your brain that releases you from the power of your obsessions, so we want to exercise it.

As you continue to meditate—that is, to rest your attention on the breath—notice when your attention goes elsewhere, and then return to the breath. You are going to be distracted by thoughts, feelings, and sensations. The key is to stay out of problem-solving the content—otherwise known as "anything at all that you're stuck on and worried about" (Wilson 2016, p. 62)—and stick to the main theme: that these are thoughts, feelings, and sensations, and *only* thoughts, feelings, and sensations. They are streams of data in the mind.

Liking them or disliking them is not at issue here. The skill you are trying to develop is simply observing them.

Mindfulness entails observing things in the present moment without judgment as they *are,* not as they could or should be. When you observe a thought, then you have done just that, observed a thought. It doesn't matter what the thought is about or where it came from, or how often you have been in its presence. When meditating, there is a thought, and then we return to the breath.

Reasonable people can agree that watching your breath for more than a few seconds is pretty boring. Remember that the purpose of meditation for OCD is to develop the skill of coming back to the present, back to your anchor. So it is precisely *because* the breath is so boring that it's the perfect anchor for this exercise. It requires *intention* to both observe that you have wandered off into thought or feeling, and to allow yourself to return to the anchor of the breath even when that may seem unimportant. It is meant to be challenging. But it is also meant to open you up to having curiosity about the banal. Why, in the presence of an OCD thought or anxious feeling, are you not impressed by the flavor of your food or the sensation of a breeze? Consider that if you were to improve in your ability to return to and remain with something noncompelling, such as the breath, how could OCD ever hope to *compel* you to do your compulsions?

Run Credits: Ending the Meditation

You can choose a specific time to end the meditation or end when it feels appropriate to do so, but start with short sessions, such as five or ten minutes, or even one minute. When you are ready to end the practice, bring your attention back to the space. End the meditation more or less the same way you began, by checking in with the various elements of the present space you are in. Open your eyes. Take a few beats to collect yourself and return to your day.

By meditating and practicing the skill of returning to the present without judging your distractions, you are likely to find that you become better at doing so in your day-to-day life. You might say meditation is "working" when you notice that you are generally responding to OCD symptoms the way you might respond to those same symptoms if they occurred during a meditation exercise: by acknowledging them and then turning your attention back to what you were doing.

This approach often gets confused with *ignoring* your symptoms, but in fact it is much more powerful. Ignoring your thoughts is an act of denial, of pretending something isn't there when it is. Mindfulness asks you to acknowledge the thoughts, but choose to respond to them openly and without attachment. We know, easier said than done. But that's what we're aiming for. More presence. More pursuit of the things we care about. Less wandering around lost, at the mercy of OCD.

Being Mindful of Expectations

People with OCD tend to approach tasks from an evaluative standpoint. If you are reading this, you are no stranger to questions like, "Am I doing this right?" or "On a scale of 1 to I-should-never-have-been-born, how poorly am I doing?" This is the hardest part about meditation and mindfulness in general. It doesn't really work as a performance. "Good" meditations are just meditations you feel good about. They don't have specific qualities that are better than meditations you feel bad about. If you are able to stay attuned to your anchor (the breath) for ten seconds out of ten minutes, then that's great. Twenty seconds doesn't make you a better person or a better meditator. The only thing to assess is simply: when you become aware that you have wandered off, do you note this and bring yourself back, even if just for a moment? If so, that was a moment of mindfulness. Every time your mind wanders and you bring it gently back, that's being mindful. So if that happens two times, twenty times, two hundred times, or two thousand times during your meditations, those are all moments of mindfulness.

You are trying to increase the speed and ease with which you become aware of being distracted and then return from it to your anchor. But if you position yourself as a success or failure based on how many thoughts you have or how relaxed you feel or how focused you were, then you will not benefit from this exercise. In fact, Tom Magliozzi, cohost of the National Public Radio hit show *Car Talk*, had a great saying about expectations that we think applies here (and to all of life): *happiness equals reality minus expectations*. Try to reduce your expectations about meditation and mindfulness; this will help you peacefully tolerate, if not outright enjoy, the process.

In This Moment

In this chapter we've given you a sense of the power of mindfulness, one that you may not have realized before. We looked at why people with OCD might want to take an interest in mindfulness; then we explored a basic definition of the term. We have taken you through some of the basic steps of a mindfulness meditation exercise and discussed how the actions you take in meditation can positively affect how you relate to your OCD. Through meditating, you build the mental muscle that allows you to bring yourself back, again and again, to the experience of the present moment. You can learn to see thoughts as just thoughts and feelings as just feelings. Viktor Frankl, the Austrian psychiatrist and Holocaust survivor, is widely credited with the observation that there is a space between any stimulus and our response to it; that in that space we find the freedom and power to choose how we respond; and that in our response lies our growth, freedom, and happiness. Mindfulness gives us that space and forms an essential part of the foundation for freedom from OCD. The other part of that foundation is self-compassion—the ability to allow yourself to be who you are in the present moment. We will discuss this concept of giving yourself a fair shot—a concept which may also be new to you—in the next chapter.

CHAPTER 2

Self-Compassion

There's a good reason we are devoting an entire chapter of this book to self-compassion: it's typically a foreign concept to those of us with OCD! This makes sense, if you think about how mean OCD is to the people who have it. After listening for so long to OCD's demeaning voice, many people unconsciously make the disorder's voice their own, and their self-talk starts to become critical, judgmental, and demoralizing. Unfortunately, this just makes someone with OCD feel more isolated, fearful, and exhausted.

But fortunately, there is a healing alternative: self-compassion. Through developing the skill of self-compassion, people with OCD can learn to gently acknowledge painful emotions, recognize they are not alone, and give themselves encouragement and support. In this chapter, we'll discuss empathy and compassion as foundations for self-compassion, the three core elements of self-compassion, how to create a self-compassion coping statement, and how to avoid misusing self-compassion in response to your OCD.

Why People with OCD Deserve Self-Compassion

We love working with people who have OCD. They are considerate, incredibly compassionate, and overflowing with empathy (sometimes to their own detriment!). They also tend to be smart, creative, and quick-witted. But the majority of OCD sufferers have one major flaw. They are mean.

What? Didn't you just say that people with OCD are considerate and compassionate? Why yes, we did. And they are. To other people. But often people with OCD treat *themselves*, well, terribly.

You may be thinking, "But that's not true!" And maybe it isn't, all the time. But do you often let others off the hook for stuff that you'd never in a million years let yourself get away with? Do you find that you frequently talk to yourself in a way in which you'd never address anyone else you cared about? Do you play down or ignore your positive qualities, saying, "They don't count!" while recognizing the benefits of those same qualities in others? Do you set a low expectations bar for others that they can easily hop over, but for yourself set an extremely high bar, way up in the clouds, that you don't stand a chance of clearing? It may be hard to admit, but you'd never treat a friend (and maybe not even an enemy!) the way you treat yourself at times.

So why in the world are people with OCD so mean to themselves? We can all, at least partly, blame OCD.

OCD Treats You Like You're Special, In a Bad Way

OCD is a paragon of meanness, and there are three ways it lays the foundation for people turning on themselves. First, OCD tells sufferers that they are special (McGrath 2006). That label might seem like a good thing, but what it really means is that OCD sufferers apply rules to themselves differently than to everyone else. (It's akin to feeling you suffer from "terminal uniqueness," a term used by some in Alcoholics Anonymous to describe those who tend to feel unredeemable and set apart from others, even in a room full of people suffering from the same addiction.) There are "majority rules" and "OCD rules," and OCD rules are always more stringent, complicated, and time-consuming than the majority rules (the rules for everyone else).

People following majority rules can run over a pothole and keep going, but people with "hit and run" OCD, for instance, must follow OCD rules and turn the car around and go back and check to make sure they didn't leave a wounded victim behind them. It doesn't matter that OCD rules typically make no logical sense and may cause more danger than they prevent (for example, driving while staring at the rearview mirror or endlessly looping the same block, looking in the median for bodies). Logic doesn't matter when it comes to OCD specialness. OCD tells its victims (and we mean the people with OCD, not the people they are allegedly running down or otherwise hurting) that they can't be "normal" like everyone else. The "normal" person can come home from a long trip and collapse on the couch in their clothes, but the OCD sufferer insists on abiding by the "special" rule of showering and changing clothes, lest they track a contaminant from the outside onto their couch, unleashing havoc in the hygiene ecosystem. This specialness makes OCD sufferers feel disconnected from others, overburdened by responsibility, and somehow more dangerous and culpable than other people.

OCD Wants You to Be Perfect

OCD also demands that those who have it achieve perfection, especially in following OCD rules. Like an unyielding turn-of-the-century schoolmaster poised with a ruler over a child's bare knuckles, it will not accept anything less. OCD *always* wants its rituals done perfectly. And yet, paradoxically, it changes the rules constantly and keeps redefining what perfect is. A person with morality- or relationship-themed OCD might feel that she knows exactly what she has to confess to her partner to receive OCD's absolution, but as she turns to walk away, hearing the taunting whisper of OCD, "Are you sure you told him *everything?*" she turns back and is compelled to share even more. She must share perfectly, because OCD rules are meant to help it achieve certainty, and OCD often conflates perfection and certainty. In OCD's twisted logic, if something is perfect, it is more likely to be certain, and OCD thrives on the illusion of certainty. Much as we try to appease OCD's demand for certainty, nothing in life is certain, except for death and taxes (and your mother's calling during the most climactic scene of the season finale of your favorite show).

"Perfect" is also unattainable. Like a pigeon being chased by enthusiastic toddlers around the outskirts of a fountain in a city park, perfection is always just out of reach. And while chasing pigeons is fun, chasing certainty and perfection is not. Perfection is actually the terrible state of being on the edge of disaster. Anything that disrupts perfection in any way necessarily destroys it. So those in search of the perfect not only feel exposed, unworthy, and incapable, but are also mired in a sense of perpetual failure.

OCD is Verbally Abusive

OCD yells at its victims, and its tone is arrogant, condescending, and unyielding:

"Wash your hands again, you inconsiderate oaf! Do you want to be the person who starts a hepatitis outbreak?!?"

"Did you just think a blasphemous thought about God? What is wrong with you? Who does that? People going to hell, that's who! You'd better think that thought over again, correctly this time, and maybe say a prayer, or you are destined for damnation. What kind of person are you?"

"What was it your wife just said? You didn't catch it all, did you? You have to know! If you don't find out, it will drive you mad for the rest of your life! Ask again!"

"You wore that shirt on the bus, and it's just gross. Eeeewwww, that horrible, icky feeling is unbearable. Make it go away right now!"

Sometimes OCD will make a snide comment like these. Other times it will launch into a brief harangue. At its worst, it launches into a running diatribe lasting for hours or days. After enough of this, self-confidence drains out, to be replaced by a sticky, toxic mixture of shame and exhaustion.

Axis of Evil

This axis of specialness, perfection, and mental abuse creates an inner torture chamber. Being "special" leaves the person with OCD feeling all alone, in OCD-imposed solitary confinement. The quest for perfection turns the thumbscrews a little harder and leaves sufferers feeling like they are never good enough, no matter what they do. And the mental flagellation adds insult to injury, so they feel drained of energy and, at times, utterly hopeless. As a result, slowly but surely, OCD sufferers unconsciously take OCD's vicious voice and make it their own. People on the outside can treat OCD sufferers with compassion, but with a bully on the inside, the kindness of others won't suffice. What's required is a competing voice inside the OCD sufferer's mind to heal and give strength.

The Healing Alternative of Self-Compassion

"When we're caught up in our pain, we also go to war against *ourselves*. The body protects itself against danger through fight, flight, or freeze (staying frozen in place), but when we're challenged emotionally, these reactions become an unholy trinity of self-criticism, self-isolation, and self-absorption. A healing alternative is to cultivate a new relationship to ourselves described by research psychologist Kristin Neff as self-kindness, a sense of connection with the rest of humanity, and balanced awareness. That's self-compassion."

—Christopher Germer, *The Mindful Path to Self-Compassion* (2009, Location 19–20 of 282)

Germer articulates the effect of the emotional pain inflicted by being held captive in OCD's torture chamber—and what we can do about it. Let's begin our discussion of self-compassion for OCD by exploring its foundation: empathy and compassion.

Sympathy vs. Empathy

All of us have offered sympathy to others at times, most often when someone loses a loved one and we send sympathy cards or offer our condolences in other ways. Empathy may seem similar to sympathy, but they are actually quite different concepts. Empathy is being present with someone while they are struggling, by recognizing how that person is probably feeling and then communicating that understanding without judgment. You don't have to have been through the same experience to feel and offer someone empathy. You only have to imagine how it might feel, based on your own emotional experience, and communicate that to the person, without judging her.

Brené Brown, in a talk she gave to the RSA (Royal Society for the Encouragement of Arts, Manufactures and Commerce; later turned into an animated video by Katy Davis), says, "Empathy fuels connection. Sympathy drives disconnection" (Brown 2013). In the video, a fox is clearly having a tough time, and a bear demonstrates empathy by taking her

41

perspective, not judging her, and then sharing with her that he understands how she feels. The video shows the fox in a deep, dark hole; the bear climbs down to join her and says, "I know what it's like down here, and you're not alone."

Giving sympathy is a little different. It's feeling sorry for something that is happening to *her* and is *not happening to you*. Sympathy is illustrated in the video when a deer comes by, sticks his head down into the hole where the bear and fox are stuck, and comments that it must be *bad* being down there in the hole. He is "up here" and they are "down there"—he is separated from them.

Defining Compassion

Empathy alone, however, doesn't take us very far. After all, a torturer's ability to know what his victim feels would only make him more sadistic! So you also need the desire to improve the condition of others or oneself, to reduce suffering. Empathy is identifying with what is going on in the self and others, but compassion is really getting into what's going on and helping to make it better. The Dalai Lama described the difference between compassion and empathy as follows: if you see a man who is being crushed under a rock, empathy would be imagining how he must feel, and compassion would be helping him get out from under the rock! (Lama, Tutu, and Abrams 2016).

In chapter 36 of her book *Comfortable with Uncertainty* (2003), Pema Chodron says, "Compassion practice is daring. It involves learning to relax and allow ourselves to move gently toward what scares us. The trick to doing this is to stay with emotional distress without tightening into aversion; to let fear soften us rather than harden into resistance" (Location 85 of 229).

Therefore, in many ways being compassionate is akin to something most of us with OCD can relate to: exposure therapy. In exposure therapy, you allow yourself to feel scary emotions, with the goal of helping yourself overcome OCD. Further, in ERP, if while doing exposure people tighten up against the anxiety and push it away, they only make themselves more scared, and the exposures become much harder and last much longer, so suffering prevails. The key for both exposure and compassion is to accept the uncomfortable feelings that are present, with the intention of improving the sufferer's condition.

The Three Core Elements of Self-Compassion

Now let's look at how you can take the concept of compassion and apply it to *your* struggle with OCD. Self-compassion builds on compassion and empathy; think of it as wanting to make yourself feel better when you're in pain (Goldstein 2012). Note that this is not a free ride to do compulsions or to avoid your ERP. Compassion is doing something helpful to reduce suffering, not just an anesthetic to avoid pain. A self-compassionate response, as defined by Kristin Neff in her book *Self-Compassion: Stop Beating Yourself Up and Leave Insecurity Behind* (2011), would include three components: mindful awareness of feelings, a sense of common humanity, and self-kindness. As we take a look at each of these in turn, we will show you how to put together your own self-compassion coping statement to use as a tool for finding self-compassion in your challenges with OCD.

Mindful Awareness of Feelings

Let's apply what you've learned about mindfulness in chapter 1 to the concept of self-compassion. To develop self-compassion, you'll want to start by observing (being mindful of) how you are feeling in the present moment. Further, you'll want to be aware of those feelings in a way that's "gray" as opposed to "black or white." Everyone is susceptible to all-or-nothing thinking every now and then, but people with OCD find themselves at one end or the other of the black or white continuum quite frequently. If you describe your feelings in a black or white fashion, you might end up with descriptions of your emotional experiences that are extreme, swinging like a pendulum from one end of the spectrum: "I don't feel anything. I just feel numb," to the other: "I'm so anxious that I feel paralyzed!" While everyone will feel these intense emotions now and then, usually our non-exposure experience of emotion is less extreme.

Finding the gray in your emotional experiences is important, because if you are too black-and-white, that may be an indication you are over-identifying with those feelings. When you are fused with your emotions, you feel you *are* your emotions, unable to stand back from them and see them from the perspective of a nonjudgmental, impartial observer. If you feel fused with your emotions, it's as if they rolled in super glue and stuck themselves to you. The trouble is, then your emotions are in charge. If they want to run away screaming, well, you're super-glued to them, so you end up fleeing right along with them. Or, if they want to throw a tantrum, you have no choice but to flail your arms and yell and scream, because that's what your emotions want. Emotions can be loud and bossy, and being overidentified with our emotions puts them in control.

The Mindfulness Workbook for OCD describes feelings as "basically thoughts about physical sensations. You get a lump in your throat, tightness in your chest, sweaty palms, and dry mouth, and then you call it something: guilt, for example. You say, That means guilt" (Hershfield and Corboy 2013). Being mindfully aware of feelings means that you simply recognize that you are having emotions. Then you label them

45

nonjudgmentally, such as "I'm feeling guilty right now." Labeling them judgmentally, which isn't helpful, would sound something like, "I'm feeling guilty again. Why does this happen to me? I want this feeling to go away!"

To help yourself step back from emotions, notice where they are manifesting in your body, which helps you see them as interpretations of body sensations. For instance, "I'm feeling guilty right now. I can feel the tightness in my chest." In finding them in your body, you're not trying to minimize your emotions. Instead, you're trying to experience them more impartially. Consider the observation of Viktor Frankl we mentioned in chapter 1: that there is a space between stimulus and response in which we have the power to choose our response. If we are overidentified with our emotions, the space that Frankl describes seems very, very small. However, if we can learn to become mindfully aware of our emotions, we can dissolve the super glue bonding us to our emotions and gain more emotional freedom.

Above all, remember this about the mindfulness aspect of self-compassion: you are being truly honest about the situation. Mindfulness asks you to recognize your obsessive thoughts as exactly that; thoughts, not threats. Mindfulness as a function of self-compassion means recognizing the truth: this experience is hard. Once you have acknowledged this, you can begin opening up to or allowing for the difficulty of some of these experiences.

Building Your Mindfulness Statement

Take a current experience where you're being self-critical, and write how you're feeling. For example, if you're being hard on yourself because your OCD has tried to stage a comeback recently, your mindful awareness of feelings might be, "I'm feeling discouraged because I'm having OCD symptoms." Keep it simple and direct. Remember, you are just making an honest statement about your experience in this moment. Hang on to what you write. We're going to add to it in the following sections.

A Sense of Common Humanity

Common humanity refers to the recognition that whatever it is you are experiencing, other people are experiencing it, too, and you are not alone in feeling the way you feel. One of the hardest things about having OCD is the isolation it causes. People with OCD have these incredibly painful thoughts that do not at all reflect who they are—*egodystonic* thoughts, in clinical speak. A dad may think he's going to shoot his child with a gun (even though he doesn't own one or harbor any violent tendencies). A teenage boy may feel that if things in his room aren't exactly as they should be, he won't be able to stand the uncomfortable feeling and it will ruin his entire day (even though he's not superstitious and doesn't even really care how his room looks). It's precisely because these thoughts don't line up with your identity that you find them intrusive.

All of these thoughts cause feelings of shame. Shame and vulnerability researcher Brené Brown (2010) defines shame as "the intensely painful feeling or experience of believing that we are flawed and therefore unworthy of love and belonging" or simply as the "fear of disconnection," both of which describe well how so many people with OCD feel. She further draws a distinction between shame and guilt: guilt is "I did something bad," and shame is "I *am* bad." The shame created by having intrusive thoughts leads to even more shame, as OCD uses the very presence of these thoughts as evidence of the underlying obsession, "I am a bad person," which is the fear at the core of so much OCD. Just having OCD can be intensely isolating, and shame makes it even worse. It's no wonder that many people with OCD have an extreme fear of disconnection that shakes them to their very core.

This fear of being disconnected from others is why many people with OCD suffer in silence. As OCD therapists, we often hear, "It took me so long to get treatment because I was afraid that if I told anyone what was going through my mind, they would think I was crazy or that there was something seriously wrong with me." The prevalence of shame and the feeling of disconnection in people with OCD is why the common humanity element of self-compassion is so critically important. Common humanity is recognizing that there are other people out in the world who are probably in situations similar to yours and who probably feel much like you do. This doesn't mean we are comparing ourselves to others—when we do that, we rarely end up in an equal position. We either seem to be worse off than they are, so we pity ourselves, or we feel better off than they are, so we pity them. Pity, like sympathy, is disconnecting, when we are actually looking for a feeling of connection. Instead, by thinking in terms of common humanity, we are recognizing our shared humanity—that we all experience pain, loss, sadness, grief, and other unpleasant feelings, that we all suffer at times, and that none of us is alone in our suffering, no matter how isolated we feel.

The trick to recognizing our shared humanity, however, is to make it feel credible. If you say, "I'm sure someone else out there is suffering right now," while that is probably true, it's too general to be all that comforting, and it can even bring up thoughts of how many people are suffering *more* than you are, an unhelpful distraction. By making your awareness of common humanity a little more personal to your situation, you can increase your sense of connection.

Building Your Common Humanity Statement

To add the common humanity element to your self-compassion statement, craft a sentence or two that captures the awareness that what you are feeling could be shared by others. Going back to our previous example, if you're being hard on yourself because your OCD has tried to stage a comeback, your statement of common humanity might be, "OCD is a chronic condition, so I bet other people who have the disorder struggle with lapses now and then and also find it frustrating." Again, keep what you write. We're going to add the final element to it in the next section.

Self-Kindness

"Self-kindness? Never heard of it!" When we describe self-compassion to our clients and explain how they can use it as an adjunct to ERP, many look at us quizzically when we get to the self-kindness part of the discussion. "How do I do that?" they ask, puzzled, as if we had suggested that they visit Mars for homework before the next session. Self-kindness is a totally foreign concept to so many people with OCD for the very reason we mentioned earlier in the chapter: OCD models being mean to yourself.

So what exactly is self-kindness? The easiest way to describe it is to think about your best friend and how you might treat him. Do you say, "Ignore your pain, weakling. It's meaningless! Pick yourself up from the floor and get moving!" Do you suggest, "Well, of course this happened to you. You're worthless! You always make these kind of mistakes and get yourself in these awful situations!" No, clearly you don't say any of that, because if you did, your best friend might decide not to be your friend anymore. So why in the world would we talk to *ourselves* like that?

Now think about the types of things you do say (and think) about people you genuinely care about and consider what it might be like to say those same types of things to yourself, giving yourself the care and understanding you deserve. Self-kindness recognizes that it hurts when things don't go your way, when you feel "not enough," or when you don't meet your or others' expectations. It recognizes that beating yourself up only makes things worse, and that burying the painful feelings by ignoring them only causes further suffering. Punishment, especially self-punishment, simply does not produce the results we are looking for (healthier behavior).

Using self-kindness when you have OCD can be tricky because you don't want to get into the compulsion of self-reassurance with an OCD obsession. For instance, say that the dad who fears he's going to shoot his child used to say to himself, "I'm a horrible father. I'm so ashamed that I keep having these horrific thoughts about my little boy." It might sound like self-kindness for him to instead say, "It will be okay. I wouldn't do that to my little boy." Asserting that he is certain his intrusive thoughts are untrue is self-reassurance: a compulsion that is focused only on reducing his anxiety about something bad happening in the future (that he might shoot

51

his son). It weakens his ability to accept uncertainty, and it functions as a form of verbal hand washing (in which thoughts of hurting his son are the contaminants). This just reinforces his OCD and makes it more likely that this obsession will keep haunting him in the future.

What would be a better way for this father to handle this thought in a way that reinforces his ERP? It would be replacing self-reassurance with self-kindness to instead tell himself, "I'm doing the best I can keeping it together with these scary thoughts. I'm going to be kind to myself and give myself a break, knowing that these thoughts still cause me a lot of distress." Self-kindness, as opposed to self-reassurance, is addressing *you* in the situation, not the content of your obsessive thought. It's highlighting your strength and your perseverance in coping with hard thoughts and feelings. Rather than saying "Your problem is not a problem," self-kindness says, "You can do this. Believe in yourself. You're worth it."

Building Your Self-Kindness Statement

Because self-kindness can be so challenging for people with OCD, we've developed a three-part formula for the self-kindness portion of the self-compassion statement.

Noticing what's right: Remembering that self-criticism is pointing out what is wrong, self-kindness begins with acknowledging what is right. If you are anxious, it means you are still in a triggering situation and haven't compulsively neutralized your feelings. The anxiety may not seem like a good thing to you in that moment, but your choosing to show up for it is. Answer this question: *What am I doing right?* Using our example about being hard on yourself because your OCD has tried to stage a comeback, the answer might be, "I'm doing a good job noticing my OCD thoughts without acting on them."

Giving permission: When you are stuck in self-criticism, it is important to give yourself permission to break free from its confines. This doesn't mean giving yourself permission to do compulsions. It means allowing yourself to feel what you are feeling, to not be perfect, and to not have all the answers all the time. Complete this statement: "I am going to give myself permission to (or not to)..." Again, using the same example, the answer might be something like, "I'm going to give myself permission to feel uncomfortable and be okay that the obsessive thoughts are there."

Inviting yourself to do something helpful and kind: When we comfort friends, we start by validating their feelings; then we try to direct them toward behaviors or ideas that are useful instead of destructive. In self-compassion, we can invite ourselves to make choices that are self-supportive as well. This doesn't always mean inviting ourselves to do something easy or convenient. Often the most self-compassionate choice is to stand up to the OCD and do an exposure. But sometimes it's just to step back, be mindful, and engage in some pleasurable activity. Complete this statement: "Right now, in this moment, I can invite myself to..." Using our example, it might sound like, "Right now, in this moment, I can invite myself to do a little ERP and then reward myself by watching my favorite Netflix show."

Putting It All Together: The Self-Compassion Coping Statement

When you a develop a mindful awareness of feelings, a sense of common humanity, and self-kindness, you have the three elements of self-compassion for your situation:

Mindful awareness of feelings: I'm feeling discouraged because I'm having OCD symptoms.

Common humanity: OCD is a chronic condition, so I bet other people who have the disorder struggle with lapses now and then.

Self-kindness: I'm doing a good job noticing my OCD thoughts without acting on them. I'm going to give myself permission to feel uncomfortable and be okay that the obsessive thoughts are there. Right now, in this moment, I can invite myself to do a little ERP and then reward myself by watching my favorite Netflix show.

Putting all this together gives you your self-compassion coping statement:

> *"I'm feeling discouraged because I'm having OCD*
> *symptoms. OCD is a chronic condition, so I bet other*
> *people who have the disorder struggle with lapses now and*
> *then. I'm doing a good job noticing my OCD thoughts*
> *without acting on them. I'm going to give myself permission*
> *to feel uncomfortable and be okay that the obsessive*
> *thoughts are there. Right now, in this moment, I can invite*
> *myself to do a little ERP and then reward myself by*
> *watching my favorite Netflix show.'*

We will explore more about how to use self-compassion and your self-compassion coping statement in chapter 3.

Using Self-Compassion Wisely and Avoiding OCD Pitfalls

How do you know if your use of self-compassion is starting to be compulsive? The easiest way is to ask yourself if you are trying to reduce your anxiety with self-compassion. You can ask yourself: "Am I trying to bring the fear down, or am I trying to bring myself up?" If you are trying to reduce anxiety, then you are probably using self-compassion as a ritual. Here are some examples of problematic uses of self-compassion and how to correct them:

Self-Compassion Is Not Permission to Ritualize

Sandra is under a lot of stress right now. Since she became pregnant with her first child, her emotions have been all over the place. But what's worse is she suddenly became aware of the thought, "I might snap and do something to hurt myself." She's not suicidal, far from it; she's excited to bring new life into the world. But her OCD is hell-bent on taking the joy of motherhood away right from the start. Suddenly, being around a knife triggers horrible intrusive thoughts about stabbing herself in the belly, killing herself and her unborn child. When she does laundry, being around bleach triggers vivid thoughts about losing control and spontaneously drinking all the bleach. This all coincides with huge spikes in anxiety, of course. She begins to wonder, "Is it cruel and unusual punishment to force myself to be in the presence of these horrible thoughts? Is it barbaric, even, to ask myself to be in the presence of a knife when I think I could lose my mind at any time and stab myself?" Her self-compassion statement becomes, "I am really overwhelmed right now. Anyone with this kind of OCD would be frightened. I'm going to hide the knives and bleach from view so I do not see them and do not suffer as much."

Hiding the triggers sets into motion a series of other safety behaviors, all of which send the message back to Sandra's brain that she is somehow a suicide risk when she is not. Safety behaviors in the face of OCD should be called *danger affirmations*! A more effective use of self-compassion would be to say, "I am having a hard time with my OCD right now. Anyone would be freaked out by thoughts like these. I am going to be kind to myself by refusing to let OCD commandeer my kitchen and laundry room. I will instead stand up for myself and have whatever thoughts and feelings come with it, because I will not be bullied by my OCD."

Self-Compassion Is Not for Delegating Compulsions to Others

Don is doing his taxes, and his OCD tells him that he needs to check the forms one more time to make sure they are correct. If they aren't, then maybe the IRS will come after him and he'll land in jail! He checks once, and then again, and then again, and all he wants to do is be done and stick the forms in the envelope and send them in! Don is in emotional pain, so he says, "I'm feeling really anxious right now. I bet anyone with OCD would feel this way. I'm going to be kind to myself and let my partner check the returns one more time, as I can't do this again."

That's not self-compassion. That's Don giving in to his OCD by having his partner provide reassurance that the forms are correct. He's delegating his compulsions. A better way to handle this situation would be to amend the statement and his own actions as follows: "I'm feeling really anxious right now. I bet anyone with OCD would feel this way. I'm going to do my ERP and mail this form, and then give myself the rest of the night off to watch football, even though I know I'll be anxious, and that's okay, because that means I'm getting better."

Self-Compassion Is Not for Neutralizing the Content of an Obsession

Timothy wants to be a teacher, and lately he's been wondering if it's wrong that he thinks little kids are cute. Does that mean that maybe he's attracted to them, or would hurt them? Does that mean that he should change his career ambitions? When he put together his self-compassion statement, he said, "I'm feeling really depressed because of all these thoughts. Anyone who wanted to be a teacher would feel this way. I'm going to treat myself like the good person I know I am."

At first glance, there's nothing wrong with this self-compassion statement. However, at the core of Timothy's obsession is the fear, "I'm a bad person." This core fear and the obsession itself cause tremendous shame, which we are trying to address by using self-compassion. However, directly disputing the core fear of "I am a bad person" in the self-compassion statement may backfire, setting off a storm of rumination in Tim's mind about whether he *is* or *is not* a bad person. A better self-compassion statement might be: "I'm feeling really depressed because of all these thoughts. Anyone who wanted to be a teacher would feel this way. I'm not going to beat myself up about having these thoughts right now. I have all kinds of thoughts, and I don't need to be certain about their meaning."

Concluding Compassionately

We hope this chapter has given you a taste of the power of self-compassion. In our experience, people who incorporate self-compassion into their recoveries from OCD find that it both reduces their shame and increases their feelings of empowerment over the disorder. In addition, it's really important to recognize that self-compassion is a skill and, just like any other skill, the more you practice it, the better you become at using it and the more you will reap its tremendous benefits.

Consider the two foundations for a joyful life with OCD, mindfulness and self-compassion, in culinary terms. Mindfulness is like an ingredient that brings all the other flavors of a dish to their full potential. If your life is a meal, the addition of mindfulness changes it from being "just food" to being gourmet cuisine. With the addition of self-compassion, you can learn to treat yourself in such a way that you can enjoy the gourmet dish that's in front of you each and every day.

In the first two chapters of this book, we've discussed how learning to observe thoughts and feelings without judgment (mindfulness) and learning to treat yourself with the kindness and respect you deserve (self-compassion) can make long-term management of your OCD a more joyful path. In the next section of this book, we will explore specific strategies for putting these concepts into practice.

PART TWO

The Daily Joyful Toolbox

In part 1, we looked at the concepts of mindfulness and self-compassion and how they apply to understanding and mastering your OCD in the long term. In the two chapters that follow, we will look at how mindfulness, self-compassion, and exposure and response prevention (ERP) work in concert and how you can use awareness of these concepts to tip the scales in your favor.

CHAPTER 3

Everyday Ways to Strengthen Your Mindfulness and Self-Compassion Skills

In this chapter, we will explore ways to help boost your mindfulness and self-compassion skills to navigate life with OCD. We recommend you establish a basic daily meditation practice as part of your everyday maintenance, using the tools you learned in chapter 1. Opportunities for distraction are everywhere, and the better we are at noting when we've become distracted by our thoughts, feelings, and sensations, the more mastery we have over OCD. So here you can find additional mindfulness and self-compassion-based exercises to keep your brain muscles strong and flexible. To do this, we must first understand that mindfulness and ERP are not alternatives to one another, but two sides of the same coin.

Understanding Mindfulness and ERP Together

You may have heard the terms "mindfulness" and "ERP" used to describe alternate interventions or different approaches to treatment. Often mindfulness is referred to as a gentle and accepting approach to unwanted thoughts, and ERP as an aggressive and harsh approach. A therapist may have told you "I only do ERP" or "I am a more mindfulness-focused therapist." This reflects an unfortunately poor understanding of OCD and what it means to be mindful of thoughts or to be exposed to them.

Mindfulness asks that we view thoughts as events of the mind and not as intrinsically meaningful. When we investigate and attempt to make sense of that thought, we call this activity "thinking." Having a thought about unicorns doesn't automatically provide much information about unicorns, whether they exist, and what (if anything) should be done about them. All we know is that a thought has occurred. OCD pressures us to do specific kinds of thinking, such as reviewing, checking, and analyzing, in order to attempt to get certainty about the meaning of our thoughts and feelings. Mindfulness requires only that we acknowledge the urge to do this kind of thinking, but essentially abandon it the

63

moment we become aware that this urge is distracting us from the present.

Mindfulness Is ERP

When practicing mindfulness, we release compulsions (mental or otherwise), and we release "thinking" and return only to present-moment awareness. "I am a person in a chair, at a computer, with the taste of coffee in my mouth, the sound of keys being typed, a sense of discomfort in my chest, and thoughts that feel like they mean something but may mean nothing—their meaning is uncertain." This is where we invite our attention to rest, and not on "What if that thought means something terrible really is about to happen and I really must do something to prevent it? How can I best prove that no harm will come to me and those I love because of this thought?"

For the OCD sufferer, to be aware that this is going on in the mind, and remain present with the experience—to observe and let go of the urge to do compulsions and thereby get certainty—is a huge exposure. Mindfulness is exposure to not taking your thoughts, feelings, and sensations seriously enough. To a person with OCD, this is a top-level exposure, not an easy way out. It is taking the risk that allowing certain kinds of thoughts to come and go might have terrible consequences that we may have to cope with.

ERP Is Mindfulness

Different schools of cognitive behavioral therapy (CBT) emphasize ERP in different ways. Some forms of CBT may emphasize the role of values, such as acceptance and commitment therapy (ACT), or the role of emotional regulation, as in dialectical behavioral therapy (DBT), but any therapists who say they simply don't do exposure do not treat OCD. As just stated, mindfulness *is* ERP because it requires one to choose to be in the presence of triggering thoughts or feelings and resist the urge to judge or neutralize them. But those who emphasize exposure in OCD treatment and leave out the mindfulness are *also* missing an important point. ERP entails bringing triggering stimuli to the forefront (exposure), experiencing the thoughts, feelings, and sensations that arise, and then choosing not to do compulsions (doing response prevention). Though it may ask the OCD sufferer to engage with the thoughts and feelings in a specific way, ERP requires mindfulness skills to resist the powerful urges to do compulsions. In fact, research suggests that "affect labeling" or intentionally describing your emotional experience during exposures actually enhances inhibitory learning (Craske et al. 2014).

ERP is essentially a meditation on a trigger. The trigger is the anchor, and the distractions of thinking, avoiding, reassuring, are exactly that—distractions. And when you become aware that you are distracted from your exposure, you return to it, in all its dreadfulness. The neutral tendency when doing ERP is to try not to feel the pain, but the whole point of the exposure is to feel that pain. By feeling that pain in the absence of doing rituals, the brain learns that rituals are not a necessary component to experiencing the things that upset us. For you to learn anything in the course of an exposure, you have to bring on the thoughts, feelings, and sensations associated with your obsessive fear and practice sitting with them.

Consider what the endgame is: to be able to be in the presence of an OCD trigger and experience whatever comes up without falling into compulsive behavior that reinforces the unwanted thoughts. ERP is being in the presence of a specific kind of moment, without judgment, without trying to change it—and that is exactly what mindfulness is too.

More Than Just Breathing: Daily Meditations for OCD

Let's look at a few different ways to practice mindfulness and develop the mindfulness muscles in the brain. The next few sections include additional meditation exercises you can incorporate into your daily OCD maintenance. The basic breathing-focused meditation described in chapter 1 uses the breath as an anchor of attention. The aim is to rest your attention on the breath and sit in the presence of the physical sensations associated with the breath, as well as the thoughts and feelings that may arise alongside it. The work of the meditation is to notice when you've wandered off into storylines and to gently bring yourself back to the anchor of the breath. This central concept, of noticing when you've become distracted and bringing yourself back to the present without judgment, analysis, or ritual, is an essential component of mastering OCD.

To become aware of an unwanted thought and in relatively short order notice that your awareness has abandoned the present moment for that thought, and to then return to the present without compulsions, is how you get the upper hand. If we drill down deeper into this concept, consider the two areas in which you are most likely to get carried away by your OCD. First, there is slipping into mental narratives about what could go wrong, but not realizing it. Think of how many times you thought you were just eating a meal or having a conversation and then realized you were thinking, ruminating over some obsessive thought. What if you could catch this earlier? Second, there is the problem of needing to *do* something before disengaging from the thought and returning to the present. What if at the moment you realized you were obsessing, you could simply acknowledge this and then return to the present moment without any preconditions? Here are some ideas for practicing this with anchors other than the breath.

Hearing Meditations

A fun way to practice mindfulness is to meditate on sound. You can anchor yourself to a specific sound, such as music, or you can simply anchor to the sense of sound itself.

A Musical Exercise

Find a piece of music that has layers to it. This exercise is best done with instrumental music, so as not to be tempted into too much thinking about the meaning of lyrics. The music need not be relaxing, though if it is, that's fine. But if you like activating music, that works too. Start playing the piece and give yourself a few moments to acclimate to it. If you begin to think about whether this is the exact right piece, that's okay (that's just how you think), but then try to gently return to the experience of the sound itself, not ideas about it. Similarly, if you begin to think about how you never learned to play an instrument, that is fine (that's just how you think), but note it and return to the specific experience of sound in this moment.

Once you have rested on the music for thirty seconds or so, let yourself identify just one layer of what follows. Perhaps you home in on one instrument, such as the drums. Rest your mind on the experience of the drums alone, as if isolating the track from the other elements of the music. When your mind naturally wanders to explore the strings or piano or other element, simply note it and return to the percussion.

Remember, this is the exact same model as traditional meditation. Instead of the breath, you are anchoring to a sound. As you notice thoughts or feelings, as well as other elements of the music, welcome them and then bring yourself back to your anchor. Meditation for OCD is all about noticing when you have become distracted (awareness of obsessions) and returning to the present moment without judgment or analysis (abandoning compulsions).

An Ambient Exercise

Another variation on this exercise is to sit in any space with any number of ambient sounds and meditate on sound more generally. For example, you might sit near a window where you can hear the traffic of a busy street, or you might sit near a fountain with the constant whirring of water. Start by attending to the loudest or most obvious sound. As your attention rests, you will likely begin to notice other sounds (such as birds, distant voices, an airplane overhead). These are like itches and other potentially distracting sensations that occur when we are meditating. Rather than focus on these other sounds, you welcome them to present themselves and then return your attention to the primary sound of your choosing. In this exercise we are using sound as an anchor in the same manner that you might use the sensation of breathing as an anchor.

Tasting and Smelling Meditation

For many, taste and smell elicit very powerful emotions and memories. Consider what you experience when you notice the scent of a specific spice that was used frequently in your kitchen when you were younger, for example. How quickly does it elicit memories of your youth, images of your mother's kitchen, and so on? The power of this sense makes for a great meditation challenge. By meditating on taste and/or smell, you invite all kinds of thoughts and feelings, and with them, all kinds of opportunities to practice nonjudgmental observation.

An Eating Exercise

Start by selecting a small edible object, such as a raisin or a chocolate candy. Let it rest in your hand for a moment and take a few breaths. Then hold it up to your nose and breathe in slowly. Next, place the item in your mouth and let it rest on your tongue. Note the sensations, the textures, the taste, the smell, all coalescing into one. This is your anchor. Resist the urge to chew; allow the item to sit in your mouth. As thoughts and feelings arise, including memories of when you have eaten this before or thoughts about whether it is healthy, or feelings of longing for an event where you once ate this item, simply note that these thoughts and feelings are arising, allow them, and return to the focus on taste and smell.

Once again, by attending to the experience of the present moment, being pulled aside by thoughts and feelings, then returning, you exercise the muscle in your brain that stands up best against OCD. You increase your awareness of storylines forming and increase your ability to leave compulsive urges alone.

Walking Meditation

It's easy to be so distracted by OCD that we lose all awareness of the world around us and the ground beneath our feet. We get confused into believing that first we must get certainty over the content of our thoughts and the significance of our feelings, and then *later*, we imagine, we will start appreciating the present moment and our surroundings. This is unfortunate. However, we can work to change this, with the right kind of effort.

The core concept of a walking meditation is that you are, well, *walking*, and that your anchor is the sensation of your feet pressing down on the ground beneath you. Walking meditations may take different forms with various levels of strictness. At its most strict, a walking meditation asks that you walk in one direction a few paces, then turn around and walk back, then repeat for however long you want the meditation to last.

A less strict version would be to simply take a walk through some low-stimulation space (a nature trail, for example, not a busy street), and as you walk, really try to notice how it feels to have your feet make contact with the ground. With each step, a new contact. Just as with the breath in traditional meditation, where you may notice the beginning of a breath, the end of the breath, and the space in between, so too can you notice the beginning, end, and in-between of your steps. As competing thoughts, feelings, and sensations arise, you allow them, welcome them, and then return your attention to the steps.

Checking In and Chilling Out

Not everyone has time or an appropriate space to meditate as much as they would like. Furthermore, formal meditation is not best used as a strategy for reducing anxiety when the anxiety is coming from your OCD. You don't want to associate meditation with reducing anxiety, because then meditation (yes, even meditation) can become a compulsion. However, nobody gets a prize for suffering the most. If you are struggling with your OCD and you are looking for a way to reduce the intensity of your discomfort, you can do so without its being a compulsion.

Grounding Exercise

One quick way to take some of the edge off is by grounding yourself. Consider the image of a person charged with electricity, wired, all over the place, and then "grounding" like an electrical wire, with the charge dissipating into the earth.

Hit the Ground!

The first segment of formal meditation (see chapter 1) is all about grounding yourself in the present moment. This can be truncated and used as an exercise on its own to help you reconnect with the present and reduce discomfort without engaging in compulsions and without having to sit with your eyes closed for fifteen minutes (which is awkward at dinner parties).

Step One: Stay where you are. If there is a chair nearby, have a seat; if not, stand where you are. No need to look for an exit, because it's just OCD and you're not in danger, so there's nothing to exit from.

Step Two: Check your stomach. Is it sucked in? Are you modeling a bikini? If the answers are yes and no in that specific order, then let your belly out. Tense stomach muscles are sending the message to your brain that you're about to be sucker punched. Relaxing your stomach muscles sends the opposite message. Additionally, it triggers the urge to take slower, deeper, more meaningful breaths, and that's a good thing, because it can reduce anxiety (Pittman and Karle 2015). Check your shoulders too. If they are reaching for your ears, you are tensing your muscles. Let your shoulders drop and send the message to your brain that your body is not bracing for an attack.

Step Three: It's called grounding because you remember that you are connected to the ground (this exercise does not work while skydiving). Turn your attention to the soles of your feet. Notice where the different parts of your soles are making contact with your shoes or the floor. Remember, you are not *looking* at your feet, or thinking about your feet, just allowing your mind to divert some attention from whatever is bothering you to the *sensation* of your feet on the ground. If you are sitting, you can then shift your attention to the feeling of your body pressing down on the seat. Finally, check in with your hands. Where are they? What are they touching? Are they holding something? Resting on something? How does that feel?

Step Four: Do a sped-up body scan (see chapter 1). Direct your attention to the top of your head and, over the course of from a few seconds to a minute, just draw your attention down across your body to your toes and back up again. You are drawing an image of yourself in that moment, in that space, feeling just that way.

The neat thing about grounding exercises is you can do them without anyone noticing. You can do them in a class, at a restaurant, even in the midst of a conversation, if you don't feel too distracted. Plus, this is a free-form exercise. We have just offered four steps, but you can ground yourself however you like. As long as the effort is aimed at grounding yourself back in the present moment and away from mental rituals and OCD storytelling, then you are doing a swell job of keeping it together. As in meditation, when we become distracted, we return our attention to the breath. We begin once more. In meditation, the anchor is the breath. In regular life, the anchor is wherever you are.

Progressive Muscle Relaxation

Bigger triggers in OCD can be extremely dysregulating. Our bodies remain on the earth, but our minds get blasted so far back into the past or ahead into the future that simple grounding exercises don't feel adequate. As a general policy for living joyfully with OCD, you want to err on the side of acceptance of your feelings, even feeling disconnected from reality at times. But if you're in the throes of a major OCD spike and need to function for work or to enjoy time with family, or if the emotional toll of feeling this triggered creates more pain than a reasonably self-compassionate person would demand of themselves, you may want to turn to a more concrete mindfulness tool. Typically, relaxation techniques are not at the core of OCD treatment. We make space for uncomfortable experiences, rather than targeting and destroying them. But if you are so anxious that you can't think straight, it can be hard to effectively use any of your therapeutic tools to deal with the episode. Progressive muscle relaxation is a tool you can use to take things down a notch.

You may recall the body scan from the basic meditation exercise in chapter 1. By directing your attention to the top of your head and then gradually down to the soles of your feet, you establish your body's full presence in the moment. This exercise expands on that. Rather than simply observing how your body feels, you can consciously invite your body to release tension and relax back into the present moment. Traditional progressive muscle relaxation may include purposely tensing your muscles one at a time and then releasing them to relax, but many may find it hard to let go of this initial tension. You can choose whichever way you prefer, but here we will describe simply using visualization to achieve the same results. Because this takes more time and attention than a simple grounding exercise, you will want to find a quiet and private space suitable for this practice.

Make Some Progress!

Start by sitting in silence with your eyes closed and taking some slow, intentional breaths in through your nose and out through your mouth. These should be belly breaths, which may feel like a little bit less than a full chest breath, but should be deep and slow nonetheless. You can place a hand on your belly if it helps you feel the inflation and deflation of each breath. This should be in contrast to a chest breath that makes your shoulders rise. It may be helpful to think of your breaths as waves in the ocean, with each exhale being a prolonged and intentional "whoosh," like a wave crashing onto the sands and sliding back to sea. After a few introductory breaths, direct your attention to the top of your head and very slowly begin to scan down across your scalp, forehead, eyebrows, and eyes. But this time, rather than building up a mental picture, invite yourself to imagine that the scan itself is taking with it some of your tension, some of your pain, even some of your OCD worries, washing it all away with the tide. When your attention rests with your eyes, imagine that everything above your eyes is just ever so slightly more relaxed than everything below your eyes, which remains the same as it was before. Take a moment to actually sense the invisible line between the two.

After a few more breaths, imagine that you are breathing into the line itself, and as you exhale, your breath pushes the line down past your eyes, across your cheeks and nose, down past your lips, and then rests at your chin. Stop here for a few breaths and again imagine that as the line passed across your face it took with it some of the tension. Experience the line removing tension from your face muscles, and actively allow those muscles to soften. Let your jaw drop. See if you can sense a difference on either side of the imaginary line, with everything above your chin feeling just a little bit lighter and *easier* than everything below it.

After a few breaths, begin again: breathe into the line, and as you exhale, imagine the breath guiding the line down across your throat and the back of your neck, and then resting just below your shoulders. Picture the individual fibers of muscle in your neck relaxing, lengthening, softening. Drop your shoulders as you did your jaw, as if your arms could just slide off, were they not attached. Notice how your entire head and neck, everything above your shoulders, carries with it a certain gentleness and warmth, whereas everything below feels the same as it did before the exercise. Repeat this behavior of using your breath to guide the scanner line down across the rest of your body at whatever intervals you like, at whatever pace you like, until you get to your toes.

To Relax, or Not to Relax?

Reconciling relaxation exercises with the broader theme of tolerating, accepting, and even wanting (as we will discuss in an upcoming chapter) uncomfortable thoughts and feelings can be a bit confusing, so let us clarify what we are recommending. In our experience, the situations in the context of OCD in which using relaxation is helpful are typically those where the anxiety meets the following criteria:

1. It's not occurring as the direct result of doing an exposure.

2. It comes out of the blue.

3. It is so overpowering that you cannot think.

If you're doing an exposure and your anxiety feels too overwhelming, you may want to work on an ERP task that feels a little more manageable. Doing exposures that cause overwhelming anxiety can sometimes backfire and lead you into doing compulsions to get rid of anxiety that feels intolerable. We'll talk more in the next chapter about strategies to change your perception of how much anxiety you can handle. If you're not doing an exposure and your anxiety is building over time to the point of being unmanageable, you are likely doing mental rituals. In this case, doing some ERP rather than a relaxation exercise is likely to make you feel better. In sum, if you're not in an exposure, you suddenly get walloped by anxiety, and you are in such a heightened state that you cannot attend to what's around you, that's the time to do a relaxation exercise.

If you experience overwhelming anxiety much or all of the time, we have two recommendations. First, make an appointment with a psychiatrist who specializes in OCD so that she can determine whether you would benefit from an SSRI medication to take the edge off of your anxiety. We'll talk more about medication in the last chapter of the book. Second, you may want to consult with a therapist who specializes in dialectical behavior therapy (DBT). DBT can be very effective in helping people learn how to more effectively regulate their emotions and tolerate emotional distress. DBT skills, which can include exercises for soothing and relaxation, do not directly address OCD, but instead help you learn to better manage your emotional life so that you don't feel constantly overwhelmed by your feelings.

Flexing Your Self-Compassion Muscles: Daily Exercises to Build Self-Compassion

When you have OCD, it can be hard to be nice to yourself, for all the reasons we listed in part 1. So we thought it would be helpful to give you a bunch of ideas for how you can treat yourself right. Choosing self-compassion can feel selfish, and choosing to do things that feel selfish can be a major exposure. "Maybe I don't deserve it. Maybe I owe a debt of self-punishment and I'm getting away with something." Being good to yourself can be scary, but we encourage you to try the things on the list, even if it's an exposure for you.

Recognize What an Achievement It Is to Overcome OCD

OCD can be incredibly disabling. In fact, it's the tenth leading cause of disability in the modern world (Murray and Lopez 1996). Getting to a point where you are working on long-term management of the disorder (as opposed to its managing you most of the time) is a real achievement. Don't let your OCD tell you it's not. Recognize that through your hard work and perseverance, you've taken your life back.

To help yourself feel the full, wonderful weight of your accomplishment, make a "positive steps log" of all the obsessions and compulsions you've overcome, or all the things you can do now that you couldn't do before (Davidson 2014). And give yourself credit for the small victories, because those have built the foundation for your bigger successes. If you don't identify yet with the word "overcome" and are somewhere else on your OCD mastery journey, take the time to identify what you have taken back from your OCD so far and congratulate yourself for putting yourself in the thick of it.

Write Yourself a Permission Slip

You may think of permission slips as being only for elementary school students heading on a field trip, but they are an incredibly powerful tool for cultivating self-compassion. Brené Brown introduces the concept of writing permission slips in her eCourse *The Gifts of Imperfection* (http://brene brown.com/classes/). In this art journaling course, she encourages people to get sticky notes and write permission slips that say things such as "I give myself permission to…"

- be messy

- get it wrong

- laugh at myself

- try something new

People with OCD tend to be pretty good rule followers, and what we're suggesting here is to make your *own* rules that give yourself permission to practice self-kindness. For instance, permission slips for people with OCD might say: "I give myself permission to…"

- slip and do a compulsion every now and then (because that's going to happen anyway!)

- be imperfect and make mistakes

- try some of the games in this book

- love myself, even if I have OCD

- give myself a break when something is harder for me than it is for others who don't have OCD

- have ups and downs, and know that's okay

- not have the answers

For this exercise, at the beginning of each day write yourself a few permission slips and put them into your pocket or purse. Refer to them during the day to remind yourself that you have permission to do, think, or feel things that allow you to experience self-kindness.

Sometimes, Go Easy on Your OCD

Different situations call for different techniques, and sometimes it behooves us to speak nicely to OCD. It is, after all, trying to help—in its own twisted way. For this self-compassion exercise, try saying to your OCD, "You know, OCD, I get that you are trying to help. And that you're scared. But I've got this. We can handle this. And I'm going to be firm and compassionate with you as I tell you that I'm not doing your compulsion, even though it's going to make you more scared."

83

People often confuse being self-compassionate with being passive. You may think, "If I'm acknowledging that OCD is just trying to help me avoid some terrible threat, then I'm making my compulsions seem more reasonable. Further, if I then invite myself to do something kind, I'll assume that means I'll choose to get relief by doing my compulsions." On the contrary, the self-compassionate move is to treat the OCD like a confused child and reflect back that it has been heard, but this just isn't the way things are going to go today. Today you are going to choose exposure over compulsion and gently let the OCD know it's simply misinformed. After all, it's just trying to help, right?

Celebrate Your Attention to Minutia

If you consider the OCD experience in broader terms—as more than just a set of unwanted symptoms, but an experience of a heightened awareness—this viewpoint can take the focus from being exclusively on the negative to valuing a bigger, more self-compassionate picture. We recommend you remind yourself regularly how your laser-like attention to details, for example, is responsible for more than just noticing what's wrong. It is also a major contributor to the depth with which you love things. For example, maybe you notice that the director of the movie you are watching used a visual style that was similar to the one in your favorite movie from when you were a teen, and you think, "Nobody else would have noticed that!"

In other words, recognizing that your skill at awareness is influenced by your OCD can help open you up to self-compassion when the skill feels like a burden. See if you can find things you've noticed or created that are clearly influenced by this type of attention. It could be a piece of music or artwork, a relationship you've cultivated, or a professional achievement. Or it could be more abstract, like your "twisted" sense of humor. Get in the habit of highlighting your good "obsessive" qualities, not to encourage behavior that impairs your functioning, but to *discourage* blanket criticism of yourself as just a product of a mental disorder.

Use Your Self-Compassion Coping Statements

Make it a habit to create a self-compassion statement any time you're suffering, from OCD or anything else (see chapter 2). And then use it frequently! Remind yourself. Write it down and stick it on your bathroom mirror. Make it the wallpaper on your phone. The more you use it, the more self-compassion will become your default response any time you suffer.

A Coping Example

I'm feeling frustrated and angry that my obsessions are so distracting today. (*mindfulness statement*) Many people find intrusive thoughts hard to cope with, especially when they have other things they want to attend to. (*common humanity statement*) I'm doing a decent job not allowing my anger to keep me from taking care of business today, and I've resisted a lot of compulsions so far. I'm going to give myself permission to be a little off and annoyed sometimes and invite myself to enjoy what I am capable of enjoying today even while distracted. (*self-kindness invitation*)

Remind Yourself Your Brain Works Differently

Sometimes people with mental disorders like OCD feel like they should be able to just get over whatever challenges the OCD is presenting, because the disorder is "mental." But if you had a physiological disorder, would you feel the same way? Would you treat yourself unkindly and say you should just "get over" whatever symptoms you were experiencing because you have asthma? Heart disease? Diabetes?

No, you wouldn't. And guess what? OCD is not just a problem of thinking the wrong things or making the wrong choices. It *is* also a physiological disorder. The brains of people with OCD are structurally and functionally different from those of people without OCD (Goncalves et al. 2016). This predisposes them to challenges they might not otherwise have, such a tendency to overanalyze and a more hair-trigger flight/fight/freeze response. You are going to have symptoms that are hard to manage sometimes, just as people with asthma are going to have trouble breathing sometimes. And as you would give yourself a break if you had an asthma attack, we'd like to suggest that you give yourself the same courtesy when you have an OCD episode.

Consider being in the throes of an OCD trigger and stepping outside of it to view the situation and saying, lovingly, "Well, looks like my brain is not cooperating right now." Because regardless of how well you manage your OCD, sometimes symptoms are going to flare up. And that's okay. Flare-ups just mean you are human. And they have the added benefit of giving you an opportunity to strengthen your ERP, mindfulness, and self-compassion skills.

Thinking Mindfully about Your OCD

OCD is a disorder of ideas. How we experience the world in the context of our personal narrative makes all the difference between being curious about a friendly universe (Bell 2009) and feeling oppressed by what our OCD perceives as an unfriendly one. Let's discuss some ways of approaching your experience of OCD that encourage greater mindfulness and openness in your journey. The disorder is always going to push "bad ideas" your way, encouraging you to doubt yourself, set yourself up for failure, even hate yourself. Here are some counter-ideas that can help you see through the OCD trickery.

Be Your Own Campaign Manager

Living with OCD is much like running for office and having a political opponent in your head. A political opponent wants to keep you down, away from your goals and your aspirations. He wants to confuse you and your beliefs (your political platform). Most of all, he spends his time mining through your mental history looking for dirt, hoping to find something to judge and shame you with. He'll take any small mistake or inconsistency and twist it into some egregious stain on your character, repeatedly baiting you to go on the defensive.

What does a campaign manager do? Well, consider what the campaign manager wants. She wants you to *win*. She has a personal investment in seeing you achieve your goals. This often means being kind and encouraging in the face of adversity, but it doesn't always mean being permissive or "nice." The campaign manager says things like, "You may not want to, but you've got to get out to Iowa tonight and talk to these corn people about subsidies, or you'll never get their vote!" In other words, the campaign manager pushes you to do challenging things (such as exposure or resisting compulsions), not to see you suffer, but because she wants to see you win.

Make Non-OCD Rules

OCD makes a lot of rules for you, many of them contradictory (like "Do your job perfectly *and* make everyone happy all the time"). You might be thinking, "More rules? I don't think so." But some rules can help render OCD's input irrelevant. For example: "Take the first of everything." Many people with OCD, especially with contamination obsessions, will feel an urge to avoid taking the top plate, fork, or lid from a stack. The OCD probably has something to say about the likelihood that the top object has been touched or has germs on it. The problem with taking the second or third object from a stack isn't the extra time it takes or the compulsive reassurance it may provide, but the message it sends to the brain that OCD's input is always relevant—that the voice of OCD is the voice of an adviser you must take seriously. Not just in this context, but in *any* context. By committing to a new rule like taking the first of everything, you eliminate OCD from the role of adviser.

For someone with a tendency toward compulsive research and reassurance-seeking, another example of a good non-OCD rule might be more specific, such as, "I don't read the fine print on prescriptions." Why? "It's written in small letters to discourage me from compulsively analyzing on my own. If I have a question about my medication, I can ask my prescribing doctor, not start down a path that ends with WebMD."

Other non-OCD rules can be focused less on avoiding compulsive behavior and more on self-kindness. For example, "I am my number one priority at least once a day." Of course, this doesn't mean that you should enact this policy as a way of letting yourself do compulsions. Recall our earlier point that self-compassion is not about letting yourself off the hook, but treating yourself as if you want to be successful. It means, for example, that on your fifteen-minute work break, instead of using it to catch up on more work, you go for a walk or get that coffee drink made just the way you like it.

Do the Thing You Came to Do, in the Place You Came to Do It

Mindfulness is about more than just being nonjudgmental and staying present. Mindfulness is the art of detecting distraction. When you meditate, your primary activity is bringing your awareness to not just thoughts, feelings, and sensations, but also to distractions. Distraction is the mind being focused anywhere other than on your anchor. In the meditation approach described in chapter 1, the anchor is your breath. When you become aware that your attention is anywhere other than your breath, you are distracted. Returning to the breath without judgment is the exercise part of the meditation, strengthening that muscle in your brain to return from wherever it went. The implications for OCD are obvious: our intrusive thoughts distract us from the present moment, and we can use meditation to improve our ability to return to a place of focus.

Mindfulness is often confused with ignoring, but it's so much better than that. Ignoring implies a denial of the experience we are having. Mindfulness asks that we actually take a moment to acknowledge the experience, but choose not to respond judgmentally (or compulsively) to it. To aid in this approach, notice when you are interacting with obsessions and compulsions in different settings, and simply ask yourself, "Is this what I came here to do?" For example, imagine being at a library and noticing a stain on a book that you want to read for a report you're doing. You have a fear of germs, so you begin to debate whether it's okay to check out the book, whether you need to wash, avoid, and so on. Try telling yourself, "I came here, to the library, to get a book for my report, not to prove I am germ-free." Or imagine, if you have harm OCD, being at a grocery store and having a thought about pushing someone in the aisle. You start to debate in your head whether you would *really* do it and whether the thought means you're a bad person. Then consider, "I came here to buy lettuce, not to prove I'm a good person."

There are situations in which trying to get a deeper understanding of thoughts, feelings, or the meaning of life *is* the thing you came to do (perhaps a therapy session or a philosophy class). But in most settings you're not trying to convince yourself of anything. You're just choosing to do the thing you came to do in the place you came to do it. This is a combination of mindfulness, because of its commitment to being nonjudgmental and present; self-compassion, because of its commitment to letting go of the burden of criticism; and exposure, because of its commitment to allowing space for uncertainty. Take a moment to consider when your obsessive thoughts and compulsive urges are the greatest distraction, and the next time you are in that situation, practice using this way of thinking mindfully about your OCD.

Use Objects the Way They Were Intended to Be Used

OCD is a thief. It sneaks into your life at various points and takes away your possessions. It starts small, with objects, mostly. It says, "Don't use this" or "Don't look at that" because it reminds you of an upsetting thought or feeling. Once it has stripped you of things you are more than willing to do without, it goes for bigger fish. It starts to tell you what to watch on TV, what music to listen to, what subjects to read about. Next, it goes after your very essence: your character, what you believe, what you think is funny or acceptable. It doesn't let up until it has achieved total domination. Unless of course, you put your foot down and demand in a clear voice, "No, OCD. You can't have this."

Use It as It Was Intended to Be Used: An Example

It all started innocently enough. Phoebe was in the kitchen with her husband, making stew for dinner. Somewhere between cutting the carrots and the potatoes, the thought popped into her head that nothing of significance stood between cutting the vegetables and stabbing her husband. He was right there, after all, just standing next to her, putting a pot on the stove. She had had "harm thoughts" before, but they had never seemed so real. She pictured herself turning to the right and plunging the knife into her husband's belly. Guilt and disgust welled up inside her. She gasped, dropped the knife, and ran from the kitchen. Her OCD offered false compassion, telling her everything would be fine, so long as she hid the knives and never went near them. Hiding the knives ultimately led to avoiding all sharp objects, and within weeks, she couldn't go out in public without seeing something that made her think she could stab someone. This led to pervasive self-doubt, shame, and self-hatred. But what else could she do? How could she allow herself to cut vegetables for dinner, knowing that she could easily use the knife to commit murder?

You've Sacrificed Enough

Phoebe has become a victim of OCD trickery. She has come to believe that the removal of triggers is an effective way to remove obsessions, but the opposite is true. Avoidance of triggers simply makes more things triggering. If you sacrifice one thing, the OCD just turns its sights on something bigger. It is never satisfied, and it has no sense of decency. But if Phoebe can get in *before* the obsession takes hold, before the urge to avoid overwhelms her, she can remember the policy of using objects in the manner in which they are intended to be used. A knife *can* be used to commit a violent act; this much is true. But Phoebe bought that knife to be kept in the kitchen. The purpose of the knife is to murder potatoes, not husbands. She doesn't need certainty about her obsessive fears to use the kitchen knife as it was intended. What she needs is to make space for thoughts about the knife being used in some other way, while she continues to destroy the lives of potatoes and their children. By committing to a policy of using objects as they were intended, she can also commit to a policy of allowing thoughts to be thoughts.

In our example, Phoebe bought into an OCD narrative that because the knife *could* be used for scary purposes, she must have some moral obligation to presume that it *would* be used for those purposes. If instead she considers that long-term management of her OCD necessarily involves making space for scary stories *without* behaving like those stories are meaningful, she can warmly, but firmly, state, "No, OCD, you can't have this. I need the knife to make this meal, and I'll make this meal using it as a knife, and if you have more to say about it, I don't mind, as long as the potatoes get into the stew."

That's for Other People

You may have noticed rules and recommendations in public life that appear to be accepted by everyone. However, some of these ideas may make it difficult for you to stay on top of your OCD. For example, at the grocery store, you may see a box of hand sanitizing wipes next to a sign that says something like, "Please use these to clean your cart and help prevent the spread of germs." That may feel like a lot of pressure for someone with contamination OCD (or harm OCD, or both!) who is better off being exposed to uncertainty than falling for an OCD trap.

You could follow the rule, if you want to. Or you could not follow it, if you don't feel like it. Is it more trouble than it's worth? Ask yourself: does following some random sign you saw in public open up a case file in your mind for sanitizing other public items you have to come in contact with? You came to the grocery store to buy groceries, not to be perfect or dwell on the nature of germs (remember, "Do the thing you came to do in the place you came to do it"). Can you look at that sign and tell yourself, "Hey, that's a good idea—for other people"?

Another example might be the conveniently placed paper towel dispenser at the exit door to a public restroom, a common feature in some restrooms. The sign reads, "Please use these to open the door handle hygienically," with an even more conveniently placed trash bin for these towels. This is perfectly appropriate behavior—for other people. But we live in a world where we touch things. We live in a world where handles are meant for hands. So whether you call this an exposure, or just a matter of policy for long-term management of your disorder, we recommend identifying multiple public "good ideas" and responding to them with, "That's for other people."

Shoulders Back

We've noticed that many, many people with OCD are people-pleasers, meaning they will do anything to keep everyone around them happy. They never want to upset, offend, insult, demean, condescend to, intentionally ignore, or be rude to anyone. And that, ladies and gentleman, is exhausting and does not make it easy to think mindfully about your OCD. One way to counter this is to change your physical stance.

The next time you think you've done something that someone else would not be pleased about, physically pull your shoulders back into the very best posture you can, put your hands on your hips, and hold that pose for two minutes while holding the challenging thought in your mind. For instance:

- "I may or may not have offended that person."

- "She may or may not be mad at me."

- "She may or may not have interpreted what I said the wrong way."

- "He may or may not have thought what I just said was rude."

Here you combine the exposure to uncertainty with a physical "power pose" that connects you mindfully to your body. According to Harvard researcher Amy Cuddy, "power posing activates the behavioral approach system—the system that makes us more likely to assert ourselves, approach and seize opportunities, take risks, and persist" (2015, p. 220). Holding the power pose for two minutes raises the level of testosterone (the "assertiveness hormone") and lowers the level of cortisol (one of the fight-or-flight hormones). Thus, people in high power poses end up feeling more powerful. In contrast, people adopting low power poses experience the opposite: they have a drop in testosterone and an increase in cortisol, so they feel less powerful.

Consider the various ways in which you do the opposite of power posing when you are triggered. Do you fold your arms, hold your breath, scrunch up your face, try to curl your body into a ball like a cat? What message does this send to your brain about what preceded this behavior? If we breathe smoothly and stand more powerfully, with our shoulders back, we are acting like OCD's content is meaningless, and simultaneously giving ourselves a boost in hormones that make us feel more powerful against the OCD.

So next time you think you've made someone mad, or your OCD tells you that you should feel guilty for any reason, remember to throw those shoulders back!

Bring It On, Baby!

Along the lines of standing tall with your shoulders back, we recommend you also adopt an assertive attitude. Being self-compassionate doesn't mean feeling sorry for yourself and resting in a victim stance. It means getting yourself back on your feet with kindness instead of criticism. Along these lines, we like to encourage people with OCD to adopt the "Bring it on, baby!" attitude. It's a little like friendly trash-talking to an opponent before a sports matchup, but instead it's aimed at your OCD, and it doesn't necessarily have to be friendly.

Bring It On! An Example

Neil's OCD liked to tell him that when he saw an ambulance race by in the opposite direction, somewhere in his wake was an accident that he alone had caused. When Neil adopted the "Bring it on, baby!" attitude, he used the sight of any sort of emergency vehicles as an opportunity to one-up his OCD: "Right, OCD; I may have caused the fire that truck is racing to. In fact, I may have had a hand in most accidents in the metropolitan area today. The police may be heading to my house right now to arrest me, and I may not even get a trial. They may just chuck me in the federal penitentiary and throw away the key. I may lose my job, rot in jail while my family becomes homeless, and never see anyone I care about again. Ha—try to top that, OCD! Bring it on, baby!"

Thinking mindfully about OCD's antics doesn't have to mean accepting them as they are. It can also mean opening up, embracing them, and one-upping them with humor and bravado.

Take Your Time

Mindfulness reminds us that we are not in a hurry when it comes to thoughts, feelings, and sensations. Yes, we sometimes have to make quick *behavioral* decisions in life, but we don't need to make decisions about our internal experiences. You just need to observe them. For instance, consider what you experience in the exact moment that you get triggered by something. If you have contamination obsessions, it might be from touching something you think is dirty. If you have obsessions about violence, it might be from seeing a picture of a gun. In the exact moment you become aware of the experience you are having, you might sense something in your body—perhaps an increased heart rate or a tightness in your chest. This expands to a feeling of anxiety or disgust. This reveals a thought like "I shouldn't have done that. My fears are going to come true! I'm a failure!" All of this may happen in the first second of your experience, *before* you even become aware that your OCD has distracted you from what you were doing. Remember, mindfulness enables us to notice when we are present and when we are not, and to pick up the difference between the two more quickly. So if you are feeling a sense of urgency to address an OCD trigger and not paying mindful attention, you may follow the sensations, feelings, and thoughts right down into the hole of obsession, and before you know it, compulsions will seem like the obvious and most responsible choice.

But if you can notice in that very moment that you've become distracted by your OCD, you might hold off just an extra second or two before taking those initial sensations, feelings, and thoughts as gospel. When people without OCD say, "I'm having second thoughts," it usually implies that they are in a state of doubt. But for the OCD sufferer, "second" thoughts often spell out a clearer, more reasonable, more self-compassionate perspective. You might reposition yourself as a spectator of this experience and just wait. As you shift your perspective from victim to observer, you might become aware of other sensations, such as a more stable and controlled breath, incongruent with your pounding heart rate. You might notice subsequent feelings, such as empowerment, or determination to stand up to your OCD with your shoulders back. Or maybe even self-compassion is waiting just around the corner to give you permission to not be perfect and not follow the OCD rules. Maybe more objective, evidence-based thoughts about what triggered you are just waiting to be heard. Or perhaps thoughts about your values are trailing behind just a moment—thoughts about how beating yourself up and doing compulsions doesn't bring you closer to those values.

Let the Faucet Run a Bit

If you live in a warm-weather climate, you might notice that when you turn on the faucet for a drink of water (right, like you drink out of the faucet—just humor us), the first few seconds of flow comes out warm, cloudy, and metallic-tasting. The water's just been sitting there in nice warm pipes until you came along. So you let the faucet run for a few seconds, and pretty soon it comes out clear and cold. You can do the same with your thoughts, feelings, and sensations. Your triggers turn on the faucet, and what initially comes out is OCD sludge. Give yourself a moment to let the faucet run. Be patient with yourself. You have more time than you think to address your experience of a trigger. Watch the mind do what it does, and be open to letting the cool clear thoughts follow soon after. Thoughts like those we just mentioned—"I shouldn't have done that. My fears are going to come true! I'm a failure!"—are just the stagnant, unpleasant water sitting in your pipes. Letting the faucet run a bit, you'll find that trailing just behind are clearer, cleaner thoughts, like, "This experience is typical of my OCD. I don't need to walk on eggshells. I saw something that triggered me, and that's okay. I can be triggered. I got this."

Always Tempt Fate

One of the most common tricks OCD uses to knock you off your game is the threat of rocking the boat, or tempting fate. If you're feeling pretty good and have your OCD under control, but then a circumstance pops up where you become aware of compulsive urge or the temptation to avoid, you might think it best to just avoid or get the compulsion out of the way and not anger the sleepy demon of your OCD. It's easy to fall into this trap. Why tempt fate? Why mess with something that could bring on more uncertainty, anxiety, or obsession?

The answer is a scientific one. The inhibitory learning model of ERP (Craske et al. 2014) posits that if you face a fear without doing a compulsion and your brain's expectancies are violated (that is, what your brain expects to happen doesn't happen), then you develop inhibitory learning, which impedes the part of the brain that thinks the OCD trigger is a problem that you must flee from. So it's important to take ERP opportunities to keep the inhibitory section of your brain alive and alert. On the mindfulness front, if we do our best to remain present, we keep our arms open to the future, which is constantly arriving. Resisting compulsions, however dysregulating that may seem, invites the unknown future in mindfully. It positions us as caretakers of the moment, not slaves to it.

Connecting the Dots

In this chapter we looked at different ways to use the lessons of mindfulness and self-compassion in your everyday mastery of OCD. We started by exploring how mindfulness and ERP are two sides of the same coin, as both ask us to hold challenging experiences in the mind without judgment. Next, we shared some different ways to practice mindfulness techniques and self-compassion skills. Then we explored several ways to help yourself think more mindfully about your OCD. In the following chapter, we will focus on how to use these skills to enhance your approach to exposures and stay in command of your OCD every day.

CHAPTER 4

ERP Games for OCD Mastery

Exposure and response prevention is a core element of developing OCD mastery. In this chapter you will find brief and direct exposure strategies and other tools for daily living. We have framed these exposure exercises and tools as games you play with your OCD, because toying with an adversary is more effective than always being on the defensive. These are not meant as a substitute for a structured ERP program with an OCD specialist, but as a collection of tools you can use throughout your journey with OCD.

The New Meaning of J-O-Y

If you look up the word "joy," you'll find it defined as "a feeling of pleasure" or "happiness." While there is nothing wrong with those definitions, for people with OCD, they are just not enough, because it doesn't tell you *how to get there...how to find joy*. Being in your head much of the time makes joy such an elusive concept. Over the next few pages we are going to go over some basic guidelines for coping with OCD that can bolster your resolve to do ERP and engage your OCD masterfully. And it conveniently spells J-O-Y as a reminder that you are as worthy of great pleasure and happiness as anyone else.

J: Jump In

OCD is playing a game with you, using wordplay, illusions, tricks, and taunts to dominate you on the board. It is banking on your resistance to experiencing anxiety to deceive you into throwing the game. But what if you turned the tables on OCD, spread your arms, and embraced discomfort? As we explore this concept, you'll learn how to use ERP "games" to jump into the mosh pit of your OCD and stop running for safety.

O: Opt for Greater Good

If you are willing to make space for or even welcome anxiety, your mind is then freed up from plotting how to get rid of discomfort. Now it can focus on what it is you really want out of life, your goals and values. Here we want to look at ways you can outsmart the OCD by shifting your focus toward behavioral goals that matter to you, and not just frustrating compulsions.

Y: Yield to Uncertainty

Your unwillingness to accept uncertainty about the things you care the most about is a major liability. But if you can step aside and mindfully observe uncertainty, then OCD has nothing on you. In the pages ahead, we'll keep coming back to this idea that uncertainty is to be allowed, maybe even preferred at times, and not eliminated.

Let's take a few minutes to drill down deeper into each of the three components of J-O-Y.

What It Means to Jump In to Discomfort

If you polled one hundred people in a room, we bet that not one of them would say that discomfort—whether it's anxiety, pain, ickiness, or some other uncomfortable feeling—is enjoyable. And you get this, right? Because honestly, when you do a compulsion, you're doing it for one reason only: to get rid of anxiety, disgust, or some other feeling you have deemed intolerable.

The FFF Response Is Your Friend

Since anxiety is one of the most common feelings of discomfort we'd like to eliminate, let's focus on understanding it a little better. Anxiety is a by-product of the fight, flight, or freeze (FFF) response. When your brain thinks you're in danger, it sends certain chemicals rushing through your body to get you ready to fight off an attacker, flee from danger, or freeze and hope the predator doesn't see you. Your interpretations of those physical sensations manifest as the emotions of fear (the term used if a threat is present) or anxiety (the term used if a threat isn't actually present) (Pittman and Karle 2015).

The FFF response, working as it was designed, creates a surge of energy that gets you away from danger and then subsides once the danger has passed. Reid Wilson (2016) describes it well: "Somewhere on the open savannahs of Africa, an impala explodes into a spectacle of zigzag leaps to confuse and outrun the claws of a cheetah. Once the cheetah gives up the chase, the impala will shake and tremble to release the leftover bodily tension after narrowly escaping death. Then it will gracefully dash off to rejoin the herd" (p. 35). Afterward, the herd of impala don't stand around twiddling their hooves, worrying about the next attack. They don't seek reassurance from one another, like, "Whoa, Bob, did you see that? Thought I was a goner for sure! What if he comes back?" No. They go, "Oh, hey, look, grass." And they graze. That's the FFF response working beautifully as Mother Nature intended.

The FFF response can also be triggered by perceived threats (that is, things that seem threatening but actually aren't), and unfortunately, once the FFF response is activated and you feel physical sensations of anxiety, it can be hard to tell whether the threat is real or imagined (Pittman and Karle 2015). Because the "dangers" of our modern world, whether real or not, aren't always as clear-cut as a lion catching or not catching a gazelle, your brain sometimes doesn't know when it's safe to turn *off* the FFF chemical pumps. So we can feel what we call "anxiety" long after the initial surge of the FFF response (Sapolsky 2004).

Anxiety is just your brain's way of helping you out, whether you asked for it or not. Consider how you even know you are anxious in the first place:

- Increased heart rate: helpful for energy if you're planning on fighting or fleeing

- Rapid breathing: injecting the brain with oxygen, making you more alert and aware of your surroundings

- Tense muscles: helpful for fighting, fleeing, or staying absolutely still

- Tingling in the toes and fingers: this is the blood leaving your extremities for your major muscle groups for the kicking of butt

- Obsessive thoughts: a laser-like focus on the "threat"

- Racing thoughts: helpful for picking out exit or attack strategies without losing focus on the threat

- Irritation and impulsivity: a helpful emotional state to promote quick problem solving

If the threat were real, you'd be grateful for the help of fear. But since the threat is mostly or entirely a construct of the OCD mind, the discomfort can be a major burden. But is this feeling going to kill you? No. It feels like it is, because getting your body ready to fight or flee is intense business. But it's not going to hurt you. One of the major obstacles people face in treating their OCD is the tendency to focus only on eliminating fear and anxiety. In fact, when we spend too much time in treatment trying to reduce anxiety, we actually play into the OCD's lie about anxiety—that it is a toxin, and if you allow it to build up in you, it could poison you. It is discomforting when we are not choosing anxiety, but *anxiety itself is not dangerous.*

For those of you who may enjoy a scary movie, notice that the fright induced by the movie might bring about an urge to cover your eyes, but is unlikely to bring about an urge to leave the theater. You came to the theater with the intention of doing something you knew would cause this feeling, and your understanding of this feeling is that it is perfectly fine to experience it. It's when discomfort intrudes in circumstances that you are not controlling that you become motivated to escape it. When we try to escape things that are not dangerous, we just end up with dangerous beliefs about those things.

How We Feed Anxiety by Fleeing Anxiety

Managing your anxiety is somewhat paradoxical, in that our natural response of pushing anxiety away can actually intensify it instead. In other words, by treating anxiety as a threat, it motivates your brain to give you what you need to deal with threats: anxiety. In this way, people with OCD often find themselves caught in a loop of ever-increasing discomfort, responding to OCD triggers with anxiety and then responding to that anxiety like it is dangerous, only to produce even more anxiety:

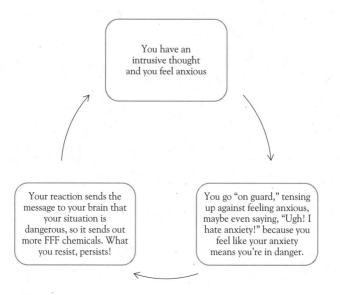

You have an intrusive thought and you feel anxious

You go "on guard," tensing up against feeling anxious, maybe even saying, "Ugh! I hate anxiety!" because you feel like your anxiety means you're in danger.

Your reaction sends the message to your brain that your situation is dangerous, so it sends out more FFF chemicals. What you resist, persists!

Can you relate to this? Have you ever been frustrated by how your anxiety seems to stick around when you most want it to leave? Your efforts to flee from anxiety only trigger it to chase you, much the way an impala triggers in a cheetah an urge to pounce. But what happens if you do the opposite of trying to escape, by *jumping in* and embracing your anxiety? You get a much better result!

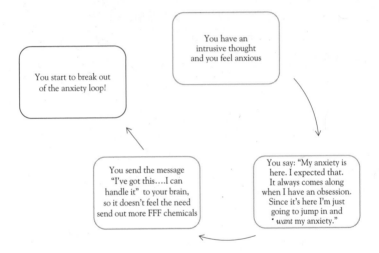

Winning by Wanting

There's a saying attributed to both Dale Carnegie and Warren Buffett: "Success is getting what you want. Happiness is wanting what you have." (Carnegie 2016). With OCD, sometimes you aren't going to get want you want (peace, freedom, time without OCD bugging you), even if you've been in recovery for years, because OCD is going to take advantage of times when you're vulnerable to try to take control again. However, if during those times you say to yourself, "Hey, I feel the anxiety right now. It isn't going to kill me. In fact, I'm going to jump in and embrace it, because this is a good opportunity to practice my ERP!", you turn the tables on your OCD in several ways.

First, you are allowing your brain to tolerate fear, which it needs to do in order to learn during the exposure process (Craske et al. 2008). Second, you are allowing yourself to fully experience the anxiety by embracing it, giving your brain an even better dose of learning (Craske et al. 2008). Third, you've wrested control of the experience away from OCD by saying that you are fine with anxiety being there. Essentially, OCD is banking on the idea that you are unwilling to experience anxiety. What if you were more than willing?

How to Opt for the Greater Good

At the beginning of this book, we talked about how people with OCD are *noticers*. They notice potential misunderstandings, potential mistakes, potential threats, and more. On the other side of the spectrum, they notice humor, creativity, compassion for others, and more. Long-term mastery over OCD is not the elimination of this special kind of mind. *It is learning to fall in love with it.*

To help maximize use of this special kind of mind, you'll want to adopt the second component of the JOYful attitude: Opt for Greater Good. As Jeff Bell describes it in his 2009 book *When in Doubt, Make Belief,* your "Greater Good" is composed of two sides of the empowerment coin. One side is your purpose in life; the other is how you can be of service to others.

Purpose

You can understand purpose as what you would like to look back on as a lifetime achievement. Your purpose might be to be a certain kind of mother, or a pioneer in your profession. Or it can be something simple or abstract like being kind to others or experiencing peacefulness. And your purpose isn't fixed, either; it might change as you go through life.

Service

You can understand service as any way in which your efforts improve the lives or experience of others. This doesn't always have to be literal, as in starting a charitable foundation. There are a variety of ways you might be of service to others. You might use your experience to help develop the talents of others as a manager in your company, or entertain and enlighten others with funny and memorable stories, or simply listen or be present with another human being in her time of need. Again, how you can be of service can change through your lifespan and across situations.

You can use the concept of *opt for the Greater Good* to find motivation to engage in ERP: For example, using purpose might sound like, "I want to do this ERP exercise because that will make me stronger and more likely to be the mom I want to be to my children." Using service might sound like, "I want to do this ERP exercise because it will trigger my OCD and I'll be able to work through this challenge so I can teach my kids how to cope with discomfort well." Opting for the Greater Good as part of your motivation to do ERP takes the focus off of anxiety reduction and places it firmly on the bigger picture. It's not just about wanting to get over your specific OCD fear. To find the motivation for the hard work of ERP, you need more at stake than just comfort. Remember your sense of purpose and the service you offer others; this can be the prize you seek. Without opting for Greater Good, it's like planning a trip without knowing your destination or your reason for traveling. If you don't know where and why you're going, how will you ever get there?

You Already Yield to Uncertainty

OCD loves certainty. In fact, it demands you seek 100-percent certainty about all of its content, and it thrives off of your every attempt to do so. This is a powerful leverage point for OCD, because it's impossible to achieve certainty about much of anything (other than the very uplifting thought that everyone is going to die someday...um, probably). And OCD keeps you running in circles on the assumption that you are unwilling to accept uncertainty. But in fact, you gracefully yield to the fact that life is governed by uncertainty most of the time; you just need to *realize* that you are already flexing a pretty big uncertainty-management muscle. You actually are quite adept at recognizing uncertainty as it approaches and stepping aside when it isn't about a specific obsession. Thus, the third component of the JOYful attitude is *yield to uncertainty*.

You Often Give Uncertainty the Right of Way

Is your car or your family's car parked outside right now? Well, you're not sure, right? Because unless you are reading this while sitting in the car, it's in one place and you're in another. Even if you go out right now to check to see if it's there, the moment you come back inside, you lose the 100-percent certainty of where it is. And please note that a car is worth a whole lot of money, and you're just leaving this metallic pile of cash sitting somewhere without actually knowing it's there, and you are handling that just fine!

Now consider this even more impressive example of your uncertainty-management muscle: do you know where your loved ones are right now? Aha! I bet you actually don't, unless they're sitting next to you watching you read this book. You *think* they are at school, work, home, and so on. But in truth, *you actually don't know* (Grayson 2010). And even though you love these people more than anyone, you are managing the uncertainty about their whereabouts with style and grace, yielding to the fact that you have no control over them or what happens to them, and being okay with that.

Another way to look at all of this is to consider that a part of your brain is responsible for saying "good enough" and accepting uncertainty so you can move on. You enter a room, your brain does a hyperspeed assessment of whether the ceiling is going to fall on your head, and it concludes, "Technically it could; no reason to think it will; come in and have a seat." This happens behind the scenes without your noticing. But what if that part of your brain sputtered or got stalled from time to time? What if you walked into a room and for no discernible reason felt unsure about the stability of the ceiling? It would completely change your perspective and sense of responsibility. When we are struggling to accept uncertainty, it doesn't necessarily mean we are doing anything wrong ourselves. It's just that the part of our brain that makes it easy just isn't working in that moment (recall from the previous chapter that thinking mindfully about OCD includes recognizing that you have a biological disorder). We then have to assume responsibility for the brain's misfire by *volunteering* to accept uncertainty.

This is no easy feat—to *voluntarily* do what we think should be done *automatically*. Most of the time you are doing ERP without even knowing it. Every day, you walk away from your loved ones and possessions, and you do it without a second thought. How do you do that? By unknowingly yielding to uncertainty and its sidekick, lack of control. You do so very well about 95 to 99 percent of the time—and about the things that matter most. The other 1 to 5 percent of the time, you're dealing with OCD content (the words it's using to scare you), and OCD is blocking the "good enough" mechanism, so of course you may not be yielding to uncertainty as well during that time. So the final part of our JOYful attitude is becoming conscious that overall you are already great at yielding to uncertainty. Let this be your secret weapon in your ERP work.

A JOYful Summary

Jump in: embrace your anxiety and change the dynamic of fear.

Opt for Greater Good: put your purpose and service to others ahead of doing your compulsions.

Yield to uncertainty: recognize that you already manage uncertainty really well, and take advantage of this skill.

It's Game Time

In the pages ahead, we will describe several different ERP games you can play with your OCD. As we mentioned at the top of the chapter, we are describing these exercises as games because toying with your OCD when your OCD is toying with you makes it a fair fight. You can do a better job of living joyfully with OCD by poking it now and then than by always being on the defensive. We recommend you think of this as a mixed bag of tricks, not a treatment manual or guaranteed recipe for success. Not every game in the box will be one that clicks for you and your OCD. Try them out, see what makes your journey a brighter one, and let that shine some light on your life. With each of them, consider how it invites you to jump in to your fear, opt for your Greater Good, and yield to uncertainty.

The "May or May Not" Game

OCD often presents itself in the form of what-if questions. For example, what if I cause someone to become ill because I didn't wash properly, what if I somehow broke a tenet of my faith, or what if I did something inappropriate earlier? A mindful way to imagine these what-ifs is that they come into your consciousness on a conveyer belt, one after the other, like widgets in a factory. But remember, these are not useful widgets. The OCD wants you to think they are useful, take them off the belt, and validate their usefulness with compulsions, which turns them into OCD weapons that cause you pain. But in this game, you take them off the belt of your mind, repackage them as "may or may not" statements, and then put them back on the belt, where they head to the trash.

So, *What if XYZ happens?* arrives on the belt. Take it off, repackage it as XYZ *may or may not happen*, put it back, and send it on its way. Remember, it's intolerance of uncertainty that stops you in your tracks. By yielding to uncertainty and embracing the feelings that come with it, you can bring your attention back to your purpose, back to your Greater Good. Try it. Consider one of your many what-ifs and practice repackaging it as a "may or may not" statement. Claim ownership of the uncertainty instead of fleeing from it.

Don't be afraid to add layers to the "may or may not" game as needed. For example, you have just embraced that your fearful thought may or may not be true, and now you're concerned that your discomfort with this uncertainty will persist. In other words, "What if I feel anxious like this forever?" Great! Take it off the belt, repackage it as "I may or may not feel this way indefinitely," put it back on the belt, and send it on its way. Further, if the OCD idea contained in the widget was or is at the top of your hierarchy, you may need to play with the repackaged "may or may not" statement repeatedly, saying it over and over, before you can put in back on the belt and watch it successfully head to the trash pile.

Mindfulness is allowing free passage of your thoughts, feelings, and sensations. But OCD can make this difficult, and sometimes you have to attend to some of OCD's challenges instead of just waving them along. But rather than do compulsion, play games. The OCD presumes you will take the bait with what-if questions. By repackaging them as "may or may not" statements, you throw the OCD a real curve ball.

Changing the Terms of your OCD Contract: The Four Questions Game

When you live with OCD for any length of time, it's easy to get used to saying you can't do things or you won't do things because of the OCD. You may even find yourself telling people, "Oh, my OCD doesn't let me watch that kind of movie," or, "I can't ride public transportation because of my OCD." You've formed a contract with your OCD where it gets to tell you what you can and can't do, with whom, and when, and presumably you get some relief from pain by agreeing to these terms. But this contract is a disaster. The terms are unreasonable. And anyway, OCD doesn't even abide by them. You do your compulsions, your life becomes unmanageable, and you *still* have to live in fear and at odds with uncertainty. The Four Questions game allows you to renegotiate the terms and write a new contract. All you have to do is answer four questions and answer them honestly.

Your New Contract

Question 1: *What changes am I going to make from this point forward?* Here you want to specifically detail what compulsions you are planning to stop, or what things you are going to stop getting reassurance about, stop reviewing, or stop avoiding.

Example: I am going to start shaking hands with people, even if I think one of us has a cut, and I am not going to use hand sanitizer afterward.

Question 2: What feared outcome is the OCD using to threaten me—that is, what *might* happen if I make this change? This part can be a bit scary, but try to describe specifically what the OCD says could happen if you made the above changes. Only use uncertainty language here (could, may or may not, might, and so on, not "will").

Example: I might get a blood-borne illness, which could be serious, and I might have to get treated for it. It might make me a burden to my family and people might think I did something immoral to get sick.

Question 3: *What is* likely *to happen if I continue to obey my OCD and don't make any changes?* Here you want to describe what it would look like if OCD said "jump" and you said "how high?" Don't hold back. Paint a detailed picture of your life with OCD completely out of control. You can use "certainty" language here (such as "will" or "going to").

Example: If I continue to avoid shaking hands and keep using hand sanitizer, my fear of disease will keep getting worse, I'll have chapped and cracked (and probably bleeding) hands, and I'll end up avoiding important social and business interactions. I will not be able to work anymore and will become a terrible burden on my family.

Question 4: What is my purpose and Greater Good (remember the O of J-O-Y, Opt for the Greater Good), such that I am willing to make these changes and defy my OCD? Describe your values and traits that make it clear you deserve to get better and have the drive to stand up to your OCD.

Example: I am actually a really social person who likes meeting new people, and I am good at my job and deserve to be able to interact with my coworkers. I want to shake hands, because that's really the kind of person I am. If I make these changes, I will be able to help more people in my work and spend more time being present for my children.

A good way to construct this it to take the answers and assemble them in a paragraph. So the "contract" reads, "I am going to… By doing this, it may or may not cause… If I continue to obey my OCD, it likely will cause… I am committing to these changes because..." You can use this format for any type of compulsive behavior you want to free yourself from. This example is brief, but you can expand your answers to include multiple compulsions, multiple feared consequences, a clear image of what life under the boot of OCD really would look like, and an exploration of your values and dreams. The point is to articulate a vision of reality wherein you are more afraid of letting your OCD run the show than you are of risking whatever it is your OCD is going on about. Read the contract first thing in the morning to get off on the right foot; read it occasionally throughout the day to keep it fresh in your mind. Write it in such a way that after each reading, your number one priority is to resist compulsions.

Getting in the Ring with ERP Scripts

Scripts (also called imaginal exposures) are a form of ERP in which you write out an extended narrative describing your obsessive fears coming true, or describing something that generates the associated feelings, so you can practice being in the presence of your fear without doing compulsions. There are several different ways to write these scripts, so don't be thrown by variations in style that you may note across OCD workbooks like *The Mindfulness Workbook for OCD* (Hershfield and Corboy 2013), *Freedom from Obsessive Compulsive Disorder* (Grayson 2014), or *The Imp of the Mind*

(Baer 2002). How you write a script is less important than what a script brings up for you.

As we stated earlier, ERP and mindfulness share a common space in which you welcome what the mind is offering and choose to stay with it instead of pushing it away with compulsions. A good script is a way to do just that: make contact with the internal experience of your fear and make space for it as you would for any other internal experience.

To think about ERP scripts as a game, think of writing out your fear as if it were true and as if the consequences were something you have to cope with as analogous to *getting in the boxing ring with OCD*. But rather than punching and jabbing your way out, you are going to let it knock you around a bit. The way to win *this* game is to learn how to take a punch. Since this book is mostly about brief exercises, here's a template for doing a short-form script. Try answering these questions:

What happened, is happening, or will happen? Try to speak in the voice of the OCD. Even though what you are afraid of may or may not be true, you fear that it is. Instead of writing *My OCD says* or *I am afraid that*, write *This is...* For example, *I hit someone with my car earlier when I thought I was going over a speed bump.* You are *not* trying to convince yourself that these statements are actually true. You are doing a mindfulness exercise of voicing the thought that goes through your head, exactly as the OCD presents it.

What is the immediate consequence of this? Express the idea that because your fear is true, something unwanted is coming next. Aim to both keep the OCD thought close and generate the associated emotions. Again, stay with the internal experience that drives your compulsive urges. For example, *Because I didn't go back to check, the police will find the body, trace it back to me, and arrest me for vehicular manslaughter.*

What is the long-term consequence? Lastly, to really jump in with the OCD fear, consider what life will look like with the above being true. Don't abandon the script by ending the story too abruptly (for example, with suicide or just saying nobody will like you). Try to write something that implies an indefinite struggle. For example, *I will go to prison, lose my job, my family will stop visiting me after several years, and my time will be spent lamenting my crime.*

This short-form script needn't take more than a paragraph or a few minutes of your time. Caution: don't do this script at the height of an OCD spike or right after you've been triggered, since this type of exposure can actually function as a compulsion if done with the intention of scaring the thought away. Instead, pick a time when you are relatively at ease, and jump in the ring with OCD just to make that contact, flex your OCD fighting muscles, and stretch your mindfulness abilities. In addition, if scripts primarily make you depressed (as opposed to primarily making you anxious), we recommend that you emphasize uncertainty-focused scripts ("may or may not"), discussed earlier.

The "Throw Open the Gates" Game

OCD sufferers who deal with moral, violent, and sexual obsessions often feel like their unwanted thoughts are violating sacred mind space. It is as if there is a fence around the mind, protecting it from intruders, and this fence has a gate that's damaged, allowing the unwanted thoughts to slip through and cause havoc. When your OCD is in high gear, it may feel like there is no gate at all. If you suffer from these types of obsessions, you likely try to avoid or neutralize these upsetting thoughts with mental rituals and reassurance seeking.

When people with OCD get surprised by the sudden and intense horribleness of the content of their thoughts, they are more likely to react to those thoughts instead of approaching them with mindfulness. It's the equivalent of thinking you're playing a harmless game of *Super Mario Bros.* and then suddenly realizing you're playing *Grand Theft Auto* and just ran over someone with a stolen car. The shock of the OCD content throws you, and you respond compulsively in a state of disorientation, not careful contemplation. So eliminating the element of surprise is an important tool in fighting these types of obsessions.

Remember, in ERP we purposely bring our fears to mind and practice resisting compulsions. This teaches us not only that we can jump in and even *want* anxiety and embrace uncertainty, but also that we are very much more in command of our minds than we give ourselves credit for. Though we cannot pick and choose what thoughts come asking for our attention, we can influence our attention to stay with or return to the objects of our choosing. In short, practicing bringing on the unwanted thoughts intentionally, as part of an ERP exercise, eliminates the element of surprise. The OCD may lob criticism and guilt your way for purposely having this or that thought, but it loses the shock-and-awe effect of putting the thoughts there against your will. Playing this game is a great way to stick it to the OCD and practice maintenance of any ERP gains you've already made. You can practice getting out in front of the triggering thoughts in a number of ways; here are some ideas:

Step One: Go to a public place, such as a shopping mall, where you are likely to encounter a steady stream of people you don't know.

Step Two: Tell yourself that for the next period of time (anywhere from one to fifteen minutes), you are going to open the gate in your mind and invite your unwanted thoughts to come in.

Step Three: Wander around the public place and look at different people. As you set eyes on each person, apply your unwanted thoughts in their direction. For example, if you have harm OCD, picture different ways of harming people willingly. In other words, hand out your worst obsessive thoughts like flyers to anyone who passes by your field of vision. If you have sexual obsessions, apply the same logic. Purposely go ahead and think your unwanted sexual thoughts about this person, that person…nobody escapes your attention during this ERP game. For those with religious restrictions that may make purposefully manufacturing these types of thoughts more challenging, it may be a good idea to consult with your clergy before attempting this game; see if there is a way to do so without overtly violating the tenets of your faith. In most faith traditions, flexibility in this area for mental health purposes is allowed and encouraged.

Step Four: Once you've assaulted everyone in your path (mentally of course), and the time you've determined appropriate for this heavy lifting has ended, stop. Thoughts may continue to come, but stop willing them in intentionally. In other words, stop driving the train, though the train may keep moving for a bit. This would be a good time to access a self-compassionate coping statement (see chapter 2) and congratulate yourself on a good ERP workout.

Testing Is the Only Way to Fail

For this ERP game to work, you absolutely must commit to a policy of non-checking and non-judging. If you use this game to test your reactions and self-reassure, it only emboldens the OCD. Remember, exposures are acts of mindfulness, so you are bringing the thoughts to the forefront of your mind (exposure) and responding with no resistance, no suppression, and no attempt to reassure or neutralize (response prevention). For this ERP game to work, you have to dive in, expose to your unwanted thoughts with reckless abandon, and commit to experiencing whatever that is like without the deceiving illusion of safety you would get from compulsions.

The Trigger "Scavenger Hunt" Game

Many people with OCD avoid activities not because the activity itself is triggering, but because the activity requires being in a place where triggers may be present. For example, even without a fear of flying, your OCD may tell you to avoid traveling because of all the triggers you might encounter at the airport. Mastering OCD is a process of reclaiming what you lost to the disorder before you knew how to stand up to it, so exposures that emphasize getting out there and engaging with the world can be particularly meaningful.

In this game, the emphasis is again on getting out in front of your triggers rather than letting them sucker punch you. Since you may already have good insight into where your triggers may come up, seeking them out and counting or collecting them takes the power away from OCD and puts it in your hands. For example, if your OCD tells you that you might push people into the street if you walk too close to them on the sidewalk, start by walking down the block and letting yourself observe people as you pass each other. When your OCD says, "You might push that person," say, "That's one." In other words, collect your triggers like Pokemon, one after the other. Another person passes by, and your anxiety spikes with the thought of harming them... "That's two."

Or you might collect noticing physical triggers. For instance, say your OCD is afraid of bandages because it doesn't like that they come in contact with blood, or cigarettes butts because they were in someone's mouth and could have germs or carry some disease. Go to a public place where lots of people congregate, and then purposely seek out used bandages and cigarette butts on the sidewalk and the anxiety and intrusive thoughts they create. Keep track every time you see one of your triggers. See how many of these triggers you can collect.

This exercise is less about trying to expose to distress and more about practicing your skill of mentally noting things as they pass. If you can count your breath, you can count your triggers. To "game-ify" it, you can practice with points. Each trigger is worth a point, and you may set out to collect ten, for example. Have fun with the process, giving yourself bonus points for kooky things, like finding a bandage featuring a cartoon character. This game strengthens your ability to not only receive unwanted thoughts, but also gently tap them as they go by without attaching judgment or compulsive analysis to them.

Take a Hike, OCD! a.k.a. Exercise, the Exercise

Exercise, healthy eating, and other good habits make living with any chronic condition easier. But physical exercise and ERP can both be very time-consuming. Why not combine the two? The following is an exercise specifically for strengthening your ability to let go of mental rituals and improve control over your attention.

Pick a physical activity that requires some effort and time commitment; for example, climbing a big hill, running, or biking for half an hour or more. During the first half of that activity, try to obsess as hard as you can. By "obsess" we mean devote as much attention as you can to your unwanted thoughts. You can do this with agreeing statements (as in scripts in which you would describe your fears as being true) or you can do this with "may or may not" statements (describing your fears as potentially true). The point is, try to make your unwanted thoughts the anchor of your attention.

Once you have the unwanted thoughts locked in, engage in your physical activity. Hold the unwanted thoughts in this way without any self-reassurance or attempts to increase certainty, and do so for the first half of your exercise (that is, if you are on a twenty-minute hike, do this for the first ten minutes of the hike). When the time has elapsed and you are at the halfway point in your physical exercise, abruptly stop the emphasis on exposure and switch the emphasis to another anchor. In other words, release your tight grip on the obsession and grip tightly to another area of focus. This new anchor can be music, an audio book, or some other pleasant distraction (bring headphones). Ideally it should be something that makes it difficult to focus on your unwanted thought at the same time.

Over time, this practice of bringing on the obsession with intensity during one activity (the first half of your physical exercise), then dropping the obsession for another activity (the second half), can help you develop a sense of confidence that attachment to an obsession does not necessitate mental rituals. You can engage with them and disengage from them without compulsions. Turning the volume of your unwanted thoughts up really loud, then turning the volume off, demonstrates that you have some access to the volume knob in the first place.

Breaking the News Game, a.k.a. Headlines

Humor is an excellent way to deal with OCD, because it takes some of the sting out of the OCD content without relying on compulsive reassurance or other rituals. In fact, using humor is a good way to help you to stay with an unwanted thought without doing rituals. By doing so, you are not triggering the negative reinforcement loop described in the introduction; instead, you are teaching your brain that you can handle these thoughts and that rituals are a waste of energy.

This game is all about using your natural predisposition toward creativity to out-silly your OCD's silly ideas. The game is simple—make a newspaper headline and subheading about your OCD thoughts. A good way to construct a headline is to say what the OCD is threatening you with in the most blunt way possible; then create a subheading that articulates how you are failing to do what the OCD says you need to do about it.

> "AREA WOMAN IDENTIFIED AS WORST PERSON EVER: Failure To Check Locks Results In Entire House Being Stolen (Including All The People In It, Who Are Still Missing)."

> "LOCAL MAN ACQUIRES VIRUS THAT WIPES OUT EASTERN SEABOARD: Should Have Taken Second Coffee Cozy From The Stack."

"ASYMMETRICAL TABLE SETTING ALTERS POLARITY OF THE EARTH: Billions of People Sent Into Orbit Because Bob Is Too Lazy To Move His Fork."

This is a game you can also play with others as you collaborate on the goofiest *The Onion*-style headlines for your common triggers. It can be used as a stand-alone practice to strengthen your humor response or as a direct response in the moment a trigger occurs.

The Halfway There Game

OCD does not like things to be done halfway. OCD is black or white, all or nothing, good or bad. To do something halfway feels just…wrong, or as if it could cause something catastrophic to happen in its wake. So this game is simple. Think of something you'd normally do all the way, and then just do part of it. And don't apologize or confess for having done it only halfway—owning the incompleteness is part of the game! For extra points, do things almost all the way, but not quite. Some examples:

- Buy only some of the items on your grocery list.

- Leave out details in a story you are recounting.

- Fast-forward through five minutes of the show you're binge watching on Netflix.

135

- Clean everything in the bathroom except for the sink, or vacuum everything but a noticeably dirty section of the carpet.

- Don't seal every opening on that cardboard box you are mailing to your cousin (admit it, your packages are taped so well that you'd need a Ginsu knife to get them open).

- Buy seven place settings instead of eight or ten.

- Say only part of a prayer.

- Ride the stationary bike for twenty-nine minutes.

This game has infinite JOYful possibilities for bugging your OCD. More importantly, this game functions as a healthy way to practice sticking it to the OCD. It's a way to build your stamina against OCD, walking that extra block instead of taking the train. Every bit counts.

It Is Harder Than You Think, But You Are Stronger Than You Know

In clinical practice we are often asked whether the experience of ERP is supposed to feel the way it feels. Many of our clients are so used to pushing the lid down on the pressure cooker with compulsions that their attempts at ERP are met with a blast of scalding mental steam. People with OCD are especially prone to emotional reasoning—that is, believing ideas to be true because they may *feel* true at the time. So when the pain of doing compulsions is shifted to the pain of doing exposure in treatment, it's very common not only to think, "This is too hard" but also "This is too hard for a reason!" What could the reason be?

1. My fears are actually going to come true, and the feelings are the final warning.

2. I'm doing ERP wrong; the feeling shouldn't be this intense.

3. I'm untreatable.

4. It's just actually this hard.

Suspense killing you? The answer is #4. At the core of understanding how to master OCD is understanding that the only way out of pain is *through* it. Avoidance is running from pain so that it chases you down. Compulsions (mental or physical) are strategies for sidestepping or jumping over the pain. But only leaning in or jumping in to it gets you through to the other side. The pain of ERP is almost always going to seem more threatening than expected, especially right before jumping in, as you anticipate the exercise. But your tolerance for this pain extends far beyond what your OCD would have you believe.

This secret truth is one to cherish throughout your treatment journey. We are all stronger than we give ourselves credit for. We are the ones with the credit to give, and there are no limitations on our doing so. So if we can carry both of these concepts in our hearts—that ERP being harder than we might expect is just how ERP works, and that our capacity for standing up to the pain of OCD is greater than we are likely to assume—nothing can stand in our way.

Bringing It Home

In this chapter we described a quick way to remember your motivations and intent in ERP, using the mnemonic J-O-Y. This stands for Jump in (meaning embrace your anxiety), Opt for the Greater Good (meaning focus on your values beyond anxiety reduction), and Yield to uncertainty (meaning let yourself be unsure about your OCD content). We then offered up a list of ERP games or strategies for playfully engaging with the OCD, using exposure and mindfulness techniques, aimed at helping you stay on top of your management of the disorder. You are as entitled to live joyfully as anyone else, and we hope incorporating these tools in your journey helps bring you some J-O-Y. In the chapters ahead, we will explore different facets of long-term mastery over OCD.

PART THREE

Long-Term Mastery Over OCD

In the chapters that conclude our book, we will explore how the concepts and tools we've discussed thus far apply to a broader understanding of living with OCD over the long term. We will look at how to navigate the challenge of lapsing and relapsing symptoms in a chronic condition, and also take a look at OCD in the context of our relationships.

CHAPTER 5

Owning Your OCD

What do we mean by *owning* your OCD? Much of this book has focused on addressing the struggle to cope with symptoms over the long term, use CBT tools and mindfulness along the journey, and maintain self-compassion throughout. You put the effort into these practices because they work and because they chip away at the self-stigma that can make living with OCD so hard. Still, even after liberating yourself from the bulk of your symptoms, there remains an unavoidable truth. You have OCD. Owning that you have OCD means approaching the challenges of life with OCD from a knowledgeable and self-loving perspective. Having OCD is not your fault, but creating a life in which joy can be possible with OCD is your responsibility. In this chapter, we explore some of the long-term challenges of life with OCD and some of the ways that understanding and owning your OCD can keep you on the JOYful path.

Chronic, Not Terminal

At the start of this book, we discussed how the duration of obsessive-compulsive disorder in one's life is chronic. We look at treatment of the disorder in terms not of a cure, but of minimizing impairment and maximizing fulfillment. Considering the absence of a cure, it can be tempting to view OCD as an impossible and hopeless burden. But this perspective, however easy it may be to empathize with, reflects an unfortunate misunderstanding about what OCD is. In some ways, the life of a person with OCD is richer because of the tools we must employ to manage the disorder.

Life with OCD Is a Relationship

Viewing life with OCD as a relationship, and not just a series of awkward dates, can be useful. Relationships have ups and downs, but a complete cutoff from your relationship with OCD is unlikely, due to its chronic nature. For instance, even when your OCD is not bothering you at all, it's still with you. You can think about it like this: you may have a sibling you're not all that fond of, because he annoys you. But even when you're not around him, he's still your brother. Knowing that you have a long-term relationship with OCD, you make decisions in the hard times, when it is bothering you, that focus on the Greater Good. Instead of relying on compulsions to provide immediate short-term relief, you rely on willingness, openness, self-compassion, and intentional contact with uncertainty to stay on top of things. Your attention to detail becomes a source of creativity instead of a source of self-hatred. Your sensitivity to anxiety becomes a source of inspiration instead of a source of depression.

You Are More Than Your OCD

There is no cure for OCD, but this does not make the disorder bigger than you or more powerful than you. A healthy way to think about this recognizes that obsessions and compulsions are natural phenomena. We can't eliminate them, because unwanted thoughts and urges to respond to them belong there. It's the *disorder* part, the part in which unwanted thoughts and rituals distract us from the things we truly value, where we seek to develop mastery. But if you're one of those who have tasted this mastery and felt relatively free from disorder, you may have recognized that it doesn't stay that way on its own. You have to do maintenance work to stay in command of your OCD; for instance, by playing some of the games we've suggested. Maintenance ERP helps you continue to maintain emotional distance from your obsessions, which helps you feel less compelled to do compulsions. It's not the obsessions and compulsions themselves, but how we get carried away by them that becomes problematic.

Understanding your predisposition to being distracted in this way means understanding that to be mind*ful* of OCD thoughts keeps your recovery strong, and to be mind*less* of these distractions increases your likelihood of returning to a disordered place. This is why it is so important when you are doing *well* to continue to incorporate mindfulness in your daily life and seek out exposure opportunities with some ongoing regularity. In other words, it's not enough to push the OCD into its place with medication and therapy. You have to *keep* it in its place by continuing to strengthen and maintain your skills. But this work need not be deflating or disheartening. This work can be awe inspiring, full of humor and bravado, and extremely gratifying.

Appreciating the Journey in Mindful and Self-Compassionate Terms

To help yourself frame this issue of OCD as a chronic disorder in terms that are mindful and self-compassionate, consider the following questions:

What aspects of my mind (my thoughts and feelings about death, sexuality, religion, and the meaning of life) will I be required to explore in depth, and in what ways could that be an asset?

It's very easy to forget that OCD denies us the joy of exploring, *without fear*, major facets of human reality that are

143

inherently interesting to explore. Cancer may be a terrifying illness to contemplate getting, but the science behind the behavior of cells in the body is fascinating. Living in fear of losing your sexual identity to an obsessive thought can be soul-crushing, but the subject of human sexuality itself is fundamentally alluring. If you struggle with religious or moral scrupulosity, you may be exhausted by your efforts to gain certainty about your role in this universe. But does this mean that philosophy as a whole becomes a pointless and frivolous mind game? No! The things we obsess about are often inherently interesting. Though people with OCD may not have a choice in how much, or when, any one of these things demands attention, they also have an opportunity to know the human mind and spirit in great depth. Could this conceptualization be the difference between thinking of your OCD as chronic instead of terminal?

How has the length of my journey of mastering OCD made me more aware of the suffering of others and helped me become a more compassionate person?

Nobody expects you to celebrate your own suffering. But if you live long enough with any challenge and work hard enough on developing mastery over it, you can't avoid an increased awareness of our common humanity. To understand one's own struggle is to be able to connect with another's. Consider that your long-term journey with OCD is about more than just obsessions and compulsions; it is also about empathy and kindness for anyone who faces a challenge in life. For instance, you might know someone who suffers from bipolar disorder. While you may not understand the ins and outs of that mental illness, you can empathize with and compassionately understand how those with bipolar disorder, for example, may be feeling out of control of their emotions, distanced from society, or just plain scared of how their minds can betray them. Your own experience can make you more attuned to the experience of others and impel you to help alleviate their suffering, if only with a kind word.

How has the ongoing course of OCD in my life led to greater mindful awareness and allowed me to explore multiple perspectives or points of view?

People with OCD must go against the instinct of rejecting their mind, with all its imperfections, and instead learn to embrace and open up to their mind with all it has to offer. Though no one would blame you for preferring an easy path, the hard path of developing mindfulness skills to reduce the impact of your OCD also leads to greater knowledge of the self, the mind, and the relationship between the two. A sunset when you're obsessing may just be a reminder that you didn't get enough done today, but the same sunset when you're being mindful becomes color, warmth, movement, and beauty in one present moment. People with OCD have to get to know their minds at a depth most people take for granted. Is it a curse or an opportunity for you? Can it be both?

Silver Linings

Here we explored the issue of OCD as a chronic condition. Though we cannot discuss the disorder in terms of a cure, we can look at the role of OCD across the lifespan as more than a destructive force. There are silver linings to having this chronic condition. For instance, as OCD therapist and author Dr. Jonathan Grayson explains, when people learn ways to master OCD, they become "better than normal," because they become exceptionally good at coping with uncertainty—not just OCD uncertainty, but overall uncertainty in everyday life (Ralph and Grayson, 2016). Your bravery in learning to master OCD can do more than simply reduce symptoms; it can reveal assets and rewards as well.

Support: What Is It?

You have probably heard at some point during treatment that developing good support is helpful to maintaining a strong recovery from OCD. But exactly what does "good support" mean? We define it as empathetic encouragement that you can stay on top of your OCD. Let's look at each of these in more detail: what empathetic encouragement means, what support looks like, and how to avoid potential support pitfalls.

Empathetic Encouragement

Empathy has four components: (1) perspective taking, or being able to put yourself in the other person's shoes; (2) suspension of judgment, or not judging what the other person is doing, thinking, or feeling as "good" or "bad"; (3) recognizing emotion in others, or being able to identify what emotion someone else is feeling; and (4) communicating emotion back to someone, or being able to express to him that you understand how he is feeling (Wiseman 1996). Encouragement basically means sharing with someone that you believe in her, that you believe that she can do the potentially challenging task in front of her, and that she has what it takes to succeed. Combining empathy and encouragement can look like this:

"I know how hard it must be for you to battle with your OCD right now, and how scary it probably is. It's probably also frustrating, because OCD hadn't been bothering you very much recently. But we know OCD is going to do this every now and then. And once you recognize OCD, you are so good at doing your ERP. I know you can do it this time, too. And I'm here for you."

Or, it can be as short and simple as, "Ugh, I know this is painful. I'm right here with you, and you can do this."

Notice that in these examples we are recognizing the feelings the person is probably experiencing and then we are communicating this recognition to her without judgment, while also sharing that we believe in her ability to do what's necessary to help herself to feel better.

What Your Supporters Need to Know

It's great if you can coach one or two close friends or family members in how they can support you in your OCD recovery. However, it's really important to keep in mind that *you can't control other people*. Some people are, unfortunately, just not good at giving support, and that's OK. But if you have one or more loved ones who are willing to try, here's how you can coach them to most effectively support you.

Share what empathetic encouragement means and how to most effectively communicate this to you. Let them know that there are some support rules to live by that will make life better for both of you. For example, they need to avoid hostility. It has been shown that loved ones being critical and hostile makes it challenging for people with OCD to continue with treatment and even see benefits from it (Steketee and Van Noppen 2003). Others need to avoid being overly emotionally involved in your OCD recovery. If they are too emotional (such as angry, scared, frustrated, and so on), they are going to add to your distress and make it harder for you to resist doing compulsions. Further, if they become emotional around you when you are struggling with OCD, you are going to start to avoid them because they become associated with unpleasant, negative emotions (Steketee 1993). You also need to recognize that watching you suffer is emotionally painful for your loved ones, so be compassionate for how difficult this request is.

Your supporters need to ask whether you want their feedback on your OCD. Sometimes family members can provide what seem to them to be "helpful" comments about how OCD is doing this or that. In fact, criticism from family members, as long as it's not hostile, *can* be a motivator for therapy (Steketee and Van Noppen 2003). However, unwanted feedback from loved ones, even if well-intentioned, can lead to resentment, so it should be given only if you have asked for it.

It may take a while for your supporter to learn how to appropriately provide empathetic encouragement, as many people have never received training in practicing empathy. Internalizing the support rules can also take time, especially if your supporter has been interacting with you differently up until now. Remember that support is not a black-and-white concept, and learning to live with gray areas is an important part of the art of a strong recovery.

Avoiding Support Pitfalls

OCD is an excellent observer, unfortunately, and it focuses on the words or actions of others that reinforce its point of view. So you need to be aware of some subtleties in how you ask for and receive support that can make a difference in how effective that support is. Not taking those subtleties into account can lead to some common pitfalls that you'll want to avoid.

First and foremost, reassurance is *not* support. Having someone tell you, "Oh, you're fine. Don't worry, that won't happen" is exactly the kind of statement your OCD lives for. Also, take care not to confess your obsession to your supporter, thereby allowing your OCD to use his reaction as implicit reassurance. For instance, saying, "Oh, I'm obsessing that I just ran over someone" to the passenger in your car is a sneaky form of confessing and reassurance seeking—if your passenger doesn't act like you just ran over someone, your OCD is reassured that you probably didn't.

Be cautious not to become overly dependent on support. Sometimes people with OCD can start to think they can handle the present episode only if they have a supporter with them, and the support person becomes a crutch, and going to her becomes a compulsion. Make sure that you use your self-compassion tools first and *then* reach out to others when you still need help.

Giving and receiving support is a process that you will refine by trial and error, just like two people learning to waltz. You will learn through practice how and when to ask for support, and your supporter(s) will come to understand how and when to give it. Recognize that you will both make mistakes, but if you are both open and compassionately honest with each other, you will eventually be able to dance beautifully together.

A Mindful, Self-Compassionate Lifestyle

If you had diabetes or a heart condition, your physician would probably recommend that you make some lifestyle modifications, such as in your diet or exercise routine. OCD is like these other chronic conditions in that if you choose to make some lifestyle adjustments, you'll have an easier time managing the disorder. Mindfulness and self-compassion are two lifestyle choices that will make a huge difference in your well-being. How can you make them a part of your daily life?

Practice Giving Yourself Presence

One of the easiest ways to start developing a lifestyle of mindfulness is to find a cue in daily life to remind you to come back to the present. Coming back to the present is exceptionally important, because OCD content lives in the past or the future. If you can stay in the present, mindfully aware of your thoughts and feelings, it is harder for OCD to make you time travel forward or backward. One aid to staying present is to set a mindfulness timer on your phone or to use one of the "mindfulness bell" apps built for this purpose. When the bells chime, it's a signal for you to stop and notice what's happening in the present moment. Some people like more everyday cues, such as getting up and down from your chair or getting in or out of your car. It's so easy to get caught up in the rat race of daily life and to miss what's happening right in front of you, and mindfulness cues are a great way of training your brain to come back to the present, over and over again.

There are also additional ways that you can continue to build a mindful lifestyle. Drive to work without listening to anything except the sound of the car and traffic. Run a quick errand without taking your phone along. Eat a meal without also reading. We encourage you to be creative and come up with your own mindfulness experiments to bring the present moment to life.

Don't worry if, as you get started, you're able to really be present only once a day or a few times a day. Every moment is a new opportunity to begin again. Of course, a daily meditation practice makes being mindful moment-by-moment easier, and even a few minutes a day of meditation as described in chapter 1 can strengthen your mindfulness muscle.

Pay Attention to How You Treat Yourself

Developing a self-compassionate lifestyle also takes work, but it is immensely worthwhile. The more self-compassionate you are, the less you sound like your OCD, making it easier to recognize and deal with it through mindful exposure. As you become more self-compassionate, you'll also find you're more motivated, as you aren't constantly berating yourself. Further, becoming more self-compassionate is built on a foundation of mindfulness, as you need awareness of how you are treating yourself in the present moment in order to practice self-compassion.

To begin, work on becoming mindful of how you talk to yourself. For many people, especially those who have OCD, a negative stream of self-criticism runs subconsciously, in the background, all throughout the day. To counter this tendency, you can use your mindfulness cues for a dual purpose: to bring you into the present moment *and* to remind yourself to pull any self-critical thoughts into conscious awareness. For instance, "I was just berating myself for not having started cleaning the house earlier." Then, give yourself a self-compassion break using one of the self-compassion exercises from part 2.

As you make self-compassion more and more a part of your daily routine, treating yourself kindly can become second nature. Further, as your tendency to be self-critical diminishes, it will become even easier to be mindful of intrusive thoughts, as they will sound so different from your new way of addressing yourself.

Owning This Chapter

In this chapter we've discussed the difference between owning your OCD and being owned by it. You are not your OCD, but it is a part of you over which you can take command. OCD is a lifelong condition but absolutely not a lifelong sentence to simply suffer through. Support is a crucial part of recovery— you are not alone, so choose not be alone by reaching out for support in healthy ways when you need it. Make mindfulness and self-compassion lifelong companions as well. Finally, managing OCD for the long term means changing your perspective of the disorder: it is not the enemy, but a worthy adversary who makes you stronger with every challenge it presents. As you become stronger, you will feel more confident that you can do this. After all, owning your OCD means that *you*, not the disorder, are the one with the power.

CHAPTER 6

Relapse Prevention

When you have OCD, it's important to understand the difference between a lapse and a *relapse*. A lapse occurs when OCD symptoms temporarily flare up. It's also called a *slip*, and during a slip you might find yourself having obsessions that try to stick around, and you might give in to a compulsion or two. A relapse occurs when, for an extended period, your symptoms go back to around the level they were at when OCD was at its worst.

Notice how we didn't call this chapter "lapse prevention." That's because everyone who has OCD is going to have a slip now and then. Everyone. And that's okay. It's just part of having OCD. What we are trying to do in relapse prevention is make the lapses as short, infrequent, and minimally bothersome as possible, in hopes of achieving an even bigger goal: to prevent lapses from *becoming* relapses. But it's also good to understand that sometimes relapses happen. Because no one's recovery from OCD is perfect. And that's okay, too.

Tools for Anticipating Relapses

Becoming mindful of slips is really important to maintaining a strong recovery. A few slips that go unnoticed turn into more slips, and more slips, until all of a sudden you are in a full-blown relapse. Except it wasn't all of a sudden, because it really happened slip by slip, over and over again. Alternatively, if you can catch slipping early, it's much easier to remind OCD that this is *your* JOYful life, and that while you are absolutely fine with OCD making itself known from time to time, OCD is not the one in charge.

The ERP D-I-F-ference: How to Tell When You're Slipping

There's a straightforward way to identify when you're slipping: monitor the duration, intensity, and frequency of your OCD symptoms (Abramowitz, Deacon, and Whiteside 2011). To make it easy to remember, we call it the ERP DIFference (**D**uration, **I**ntensity, **F**requency), as this relapse prevention tool will help you know when doing an ERP game will really *make* a difference. Let's explore each of the three parts of the tool in turn.

Duration

Duration refers to the length of time an obsession appears stuck in your mind. If you have a fleeting thought—such as "Did I really turn the garden hose off this morning?"—that disappears within a few seconds or minutes, that's not a big deal. Everyone with OCD is going to have their fair share of those. In fact, people without OCD have these thoughts, too. But when an obsession pops into your mind and becomes firmly lodged there for half an hour, an hour, half the day, or the entire day (or longer)—that's a signal that you're slipping. For instance, if that garden hose thought is now interrupting your afternoon meeting, and you are wondering whether you should call your retired neighbor to have him check whether it's really on, that's a sign that the thought is going on too long and you are most likely in the midst of a slip.

Intensity

Intensity refers to how much anxiety or discomfort an obsession gives you when you are in its presence. If the thought, "I might want to grab that letter opener and harm my coworker," comes to your mind as your coworker walks by your desk, and it causes only the slightest twinge, then that's not a big deal. That's just life with OCD, and you can smile at it and get back to work. But if you get that instant adrenaline rush, where you feel all your worst anxiety symptoms—your stomach drops, your face flushes, you feel like you just might throw up, and so on—all at the same time, then that thought is still packing the proverbial punch. That type of intense anxiety or discomfort means that OCD's content still has a hold on you. Unless you take quick corrective action with an ERP game, you'll find yourself skidding and sliding on OCD's black ice.

Frequency

Frequency refers to how often you notice a particular obsession. Say you read the newspaper each morning, and every once in a while your OCD pipes up and says, "Did you really understand what you just read?" and you just keep on reading, flipping to the next section. That's fine. That's OCD just testing the waters. But if OCD starts asking you this question each day, ratcheting up the feared consequences each time ("What if you vote for the wrong person because you don't really understand this issue, and that person raises taxes, and then you'll owe extra money just because you weren't paying attention to what you read!"), then you are heading down OCD's not-so-fun water slide.

Or, you begin to notice that OCD is chiming in about all sorts of things in the span of an afternoon: "Was that a bump you just ran over, or the neighbor's dog?... You're not going to leave that picture hanging crooked, are you? Ick, it's just wrong!… Do you think you offended Lisa when you asked about her mother today? She seemed sort of cold at the end of lunch… Did that rug already have a wrinkle in it or did I do that? What if someone trips over it and falls and I'm held liable?" A frequent stream of unrelated obsessions within a short period is another indicator that you're slipping and it's time for decisive action to remind OCD that you are in charge.

Mindfully Monitoring the Signs of Relapse

It's most effective to use your mindfulness skills to keep mental notes about the duration, intensity, and frequency of your obsessions. You certainly can also write them down or track them in your phone, but be conscious of any tendency to over-monitor or compulsively track everything. More importantly, you want to mindfully observe what your OCD is doing. Notice how often it's commenting on things, how long its running commentary runs on, and how insistent it is that you do something. In spy shows on TV, agencies often monitor online "chatter" of people who are potential threats; mindfully observing your OCD is like watching its chatter. When the duration, intensity, or frequency of intrusive thoughts begin to noticeably increase, it's a good idea to get into ERP mode. If you experience two or three of the three signs escalating, it's definitely game time!

By "monitoring," we aren't suggesting that you become hypervigilant to notice OCD's every move, which sometimes happens to people early in recovery. They feel so much better that they just don't want OCD to ever bother them again. But it *is* going to bother you sometimes. That's what it does. We don't want you to feel traumatized, just waiting for when it's going to strike next—that's the very opposite of JOYful living! Practice mindfully noticing it, making mental notes using the ERP DIFference, and tell yourself, "Hey, I'm just keeping a mindful eye on the chatter. I know OCD will try to bother me at some point, but I've got a strong recovery and the skills to deal with OCD when it does pop up. I don't want to be all worked up about this, because then I'm acting the way the OCD wants me to. It's cool, OCD. Come back when you want to. I'm just being mindful of your chatter so that I have a welcome gift/ERP game ready for you." Then, when it comes back, you'll be ready to take appropriate action.

Five Steps to Digging Yourself Out of a Crash

Well, you did everything right. You took your medication as prescribed, you saw your therapist and brushed up on your CBT tools, used the ERP DIFference, upped your meditation game, exercised more, ate healthier, connected with your support group, reread this book you're holding in your hands right now—and still, you crashed. You're on the floor in a fetal position being repeatedly kicked by your OCD, and now even the OCD is bored with it. So now what? How do you pick yourself up off the floor when you feel so stuck?

The first time you had your life chopped up and handed to you on a platter by the OCD, you didn't know what you'd done to deserve it. You might not have even known you had OCD. You just thought you were losing your mind. But as you stand there in the relapse hole, it's important to recognize that starting from scratch must include also having amnesia. Wait—this is impossible, because you can't *not* know you have OCD. True! So that means you're never starting back at square one. Don't let your OCD negate all the work you've done and all the knowledge you've gained just because you're in a difficult spot. You do great work in difficult times, and you will get back on top. Experiencing a relapse can feel like being at the bottom of a deep, dark well. Fortunately, however, this well is equipped with a ladder that has five firm steps you can use to find your way back to level ground.

One: Brushing Off the Dirt

Self-criticism can be a major barrier to getting back out of the hole from an OCD relapse. All of the questions—such as "How did I find myself back here again? Where did I go wrong? Why does this keep happening?"—can be distilled to "What is wrong with me?" This is a nonstarter. Nothing is "wrong" with you. You have OCD, and OCD is mean and crafty, and it is going to bring you down from time to time. Before you can get a better grip on the tools that keep you in command, you have to brush off the self-criticism with self-compassion. Digging yourself out of the hole your OCD put you in isn't all about exposures. The first thing to address is how you are treating yourself. If you are focused on self-hatred and self-abuse, then you are not focused on the climb ahead.

Two: Accepting Where You Are

In part 1 of this book we discussed how the first step to self-compassionate coping is mindfulness. So once you've brushed the dirt off your shoulders, it's time to take a look around and mindfully accept the position you are in. People often confuse acceptance with simply allowing things that are bad to persist. But acceptance is actually the initiator of change. If you see that you've gotten out of shape, it isn't motivating to try to squeeze into pants that don't fit. What you get from that is just more self-criticism and the desire to escape—into ice cream. If, on the other hand, you buy pants that actually fit, nice pants that look really good on you as you are *now*, you'll start treating yourself better. This leads to making healthier choices overall. The same is true in OCD. If you deny that things have gotten hard, you'll just keep punishing yourself. But if you accept that things are the way they are, your attention is freed to focus on getting back on track.

Three: Getting Support

Now that you've switched to self-compassion mode and acknowledged that things have gotten rough with your OCD, it's time to call in the troops and up your support game. You're not alone, so don't be alone. If you're not yet up for one-on-one discussion, you might start by making contact with an online support group. Or maybe you have a support buddy who knows you well enough to have seen you here before. That means they also know you well enough to remind you that you've gotten out of this before. And of course, reach out to your therapist if you have one. It's not about your therapist telling you what you already know and making you feel bad about it. It's about getting back to the work with confidence.

Four: Changing the Most Changeable Right Now

Hard times in OCD don't always mean doing the hardest exposures. It's fine if you can meet the OCD head on, but if you're climbing out of the relapse hole, it's also fine to just work on what you know you're ready to work on. If you're struggling with contamination obsessions, for example, and you feel overwhelmed by all of the urges to wash, you might not be ready to touch the dirtiest thing you can find and then resist washing. But maybe you can commit today to using just one pump of soap instead of the five OCD wants you to use. At this stage, what you need is a little taste of success. Setting the goals too high means you're likely to get kicked back down into the hole and start self-criticizing again, calling yourself a failure. Do exposure at a level that is challenging, but likely to empower you, not the OCD.

Five: No Looking Back

The character Don Draper on the show *Mad Men* had a great response to someone asking him to rehash the past: "I move in one direction. Forward." Once you get the mindfulness and ERP tools back in action, keep yourself focused on reclaiming whatever OCD stole from you in this latest battle. If you let the shame of having a relapse pull you backward, focusing on "I can't believe I let myself get that bad again," the outcome is predictable. What happened is what happened, and you have the power to get back on top of this thing. It's up to you if you want to keep score and count your lapses as failures—but we don't recommend it. We recommend congratulating yourself for learning from each stumble along the path.

Staying the Course

Lapses are going to happen, and, left unchecked, they unfortunately can turn into relapses. But using the ERP DIFference to monitor OCD's chatter can help you identify when OCD is throwing spaghetti against the wall, testing what content might "stick" and get your attention, and when it's using more strategic moves to slowly but surely get you doing compulsions again so that it can stage a comeback. By becoming mindfully aware of what your OCD is doing, you'll become more attuned to whether letting it be or taking a more assertive stance (such as playing an ERP game) would be to your advantage. However, you know what they say about the best-laid plans! Sometimes, regardless of how hard you've worked on your recovery, OCD can prevail. During these times, focusing on self-compassion, acceptance, support, and doing manageable exposures is the best way to get back on track.

CHAPTER 7

The OCD Ecosystem

You and your OCD don't exist in a vacuum. You're part of a system that impacts and is impacted by your relationships with other components of the system. For instance, you are part of a family. You may have a therapist and/or take medication. If you're like a majority of people with OCD, you've also experienced depression at some point during your journey. Stress, sleep issues, and substance use or abuse can also be part of the interconnected web that you inhabit. Each of the players in this system has an impact on each of the others, and the more you understand each of them, their interdependence, and their impact on your OCD, the more resilient you will be in your long-term recovery.

OCD and the Family System

One of the rewards of mastering OCD can be much-improved family relationships. It's worth reviewing a few key points about how OCD affects the family system, because OCD can continue to affect your family, even when you're in recovery. After this quick review, we'll talk about how to educate your family about OCD, to help you to empower your family to become knowledgeable, engaged participants in your recovery, strengthening this crucial part of your ecosystem. For a more comprehensive review of how to navigate OCD within the family, see *When a Family Member Has OCD* (Hershfield 2015).

Accommodations Are All In the Family

It's an understatement to say that OCD can be highly disruptive to the family system. People with OCD tend to obtain what are called *accommodations* from others in their family. In fact, an estimated 62 to 100 percent of caregivers provide accommodations to their loved ones with OCD (Renshaw, Steketee, and Chambless 2005). These accommodations include helping the person with OCD to perform compulsions or avoid triggers, turning a blind eye to compulsive behavior, and giving reassurance that compulsions have been done "correctly" or that the feared outcome won't happen. Unfortunately, treatment suffers when families accommodate, because, for all intents and purposes, accommodations are really compulsions done for the sufferer by or with assistance from other people, which just reinforces the OCD (see the description of negative reinforcement in the introduction to this book).

Whether a compulsion is done by the person who has OCD, or by or with help from someone else, it keeps the sufferer from getting better. Paradoxically, even if a family member feels good about helping their loved one with OCD do compulsions (so that she doesn't suffer) and even if the loved one feels better in the short term (because the accommodation reduced her discomfort), the accommodation just causes more suffering. The loved one's OCD is now strengthened, and the family is now trapped with the sufferer in a cycle of OCD.

Educating Your Loved Ones

So much about OCD is counterintuitive that it's essential to educate your family members about OCD and how they can support you in your recovery. Here is a summary of key topics you can use to educate your family:

- Help your loved ones understand what OCD is and what it is not (as the general public has many misconceptions about OCD). Don't fall prey to the OCD trap that your family member needs to 100 percent understand you and your OCD. Use your mindfulness skills to accept that perfect understanding isn't possible or even advantageous in any relationship.

- Help them understand what they can about your OCD, sharing only as much as you feel comfortable sharing. (Be self-compassionate if you don't feel like telling them everything—that's completely normal and okay!) Give them an overview of the general types of things that have bothered your OCD in the past. Or if the content is too difficult to talk about, simply share with them how upsetting thoughts get stuck in your head and how it makes you feel.

- Help them understand ERP. Explain what exposure and response prevention is, using an example of exposures you've done if possible, and share with them games from this book that you use to help keep your recovery strong. Let them know what exposures they can collaborate with you on.

- Help them stop accommodating. Explain what accommodations are, how they reinforce the OCD cycle, and what types of accommodations you used to ask for but don't need anymore.

- Help them be more supportive. Tell them specifically how they can best support you in your recovery. Give them resources (such as Support: What Is It? in chapter 5) that reinforce healthy OCD support.

New, Old, and Changing Relationships with Therapists

If you have access to a therapist who specializes in OCD, we recommend that you incorporate professional help into your journey. Even if your symptoms are well under control, it's helpful to have another person in your life who is focused firmly on your OCD. Your relationship with your therapist is complex and important. This stranger is invited into your family system and works with you to create change. These changes that you engage in under the therapist's guidance in turn cause a ripple effect, touching everyone else you're connected with.

If you've never been in therapy and are considering it now, we recommend you carefully seek out someone with experience in CBT/ERP and not just someone who says she treats OCD among a long list of other things. A therapist with this experience will know what to ask, and your job is to open up and tell the truth about your experience. This means the first meeting with the therapist may be one of your hardest exposures. But rest assured that those of us trained in treating OCD for any period of time quickly hear it all, and you can expect some relief in hearing, "Oh, that; yes, that's very common in OCD. I've treated that before. We can tackle this."

The Therapist's Role

Over time, the relationship with a therapist can become very strong. Having any person in your life know that much about you and guide you through the darkest of times can bring up a lot of feelings. It's important to address these feelings directly in your therapy so the OCD doesn't go after them. It's not unusual for an OCD sufferer to ruminate over the relationship with the therapist, want reassurance about how the therapist views him, feel dependent on the therapist, and even have thoughts and feelings about the therapist that seem inappropriate (such as sexual or romantic thoughts and feelings). Remembering your self-compassion tools is important here. You are not weird or gross for having "issues" with your "issues doctor."

As you move into recovery, you may continue regularly with your therapist or you may taper down sessions to be so infrequent that the therapist functions as more of a mechanic (you drop in every few months to have the therapist take a look at what's making that noise). Booster sessions (occasional drop-ins to brush up on your tools) are a sign not of weakness, but of mastery. Just as a car aficionado can *feel* when a tune-up might be in order, a mindfully aware OCD sufferer can be better prepared by anticipating a slide backward.

For some, the relationship with a therapist may become somewhat stale over time. This person knows everything about you, you argue, so who wants to go back just to hear what you already know she will say? You might say to yourself, "I know what my therapist is going to say. 'Recognize these thoughts as OCD. Stop doing compulsions, blah blah blah.'" But we encourage you to be skeptical of this line of thinking. If your OCD can keep you away from your therapist with this kind of cynicism, it can prevent you from getting the very tune-up you may need to prevent a blow-out down the road. Thoughts like "What a waste it would be to hear what I already know" can easily be an OCD trap to keep you off track with your OCD.

Knowing When to Reach Out and Check In

It is often said that the goal of a good OCD therapist is to teach you how to be your own therapist. This is only somewhat true. Just as a family member can't be your therapist because of the differences between these special relationships, we suggest that you also cannot really be your own therapist. Self-compassion and mindfulness can teach you to be your own advocate, stand up for yourself, and be an observer and master of your OCD, but this is not the same thing as being your own clinician. It's up to you to decide exactly where to draw the line on this. Of course, we encourage developing your own exposure exercises and sharpening your CBT tools to be tailor-made for you. But this doesn't mean you have to go it alone or you're cheating by utilizing your therapist, no matter how far down the road you are. For those of you who see yourselves as post-treatment survivors, here are some questions that may help:

- Are my go-to CBT, ERP, and mindfulness tools producing reliable therapeutic results?

- Though I can anticipate what my therapist is likely to say, is it possible that he may have a different perspective or may have come across a new technique that could benefit me and get me back on track?

- Could the voice in my head telling me I have to do this alone be influenced by my OCD in such a way that I can't see clearly right now?

Wherever you are in the journey, whether it is pretreatment, beginning treatment, in treatment, or post-treatment, it can be helpful to remember that you exist in a system, and treatment providers are a part of that system. They are not outsiders in a true sense, but rather engaged in a series of interactions between you and your OCD. Navigating this is not always easy, but recognizing that it is not easy can be the first step toward self-compassion. We also caution you against completely crediting the therapist with your success. OCD cringes at the sight of you beaming proudly over freedom from your obsessions and compulsions. Try to find a balance wherein you can be mindful of both your gratitude for the guidance of your therapist and your commitment and perseverance in actually doing the work to master your OCD.

Living Joyfully with Medication

The first thing to know about medication, whether you take it or not, is that its purpose is to make CBT/ERP more effective for you. For some, medication can improve the effectiveness of CBT/ERP in a number of ways. It can give you better access to your CBT/ERP and mindfulness tools so you can use them more effectively. If exposures are too hard because they throw you into panic mode too quickly, then learning cannot take place and the exposures will be ineffective. Medication can help keep you out of the panic zone. If exposures are too hard because you can't find the motivation to do your exercises and stand up to your OCD, then depression may be impeding your progress. Medication may help you stay above the depression threshold. If you are doing your exposure work, but keep getting hammered by intense intrusive thinking that leads you to go back and do compulsions, rendering the exposures ineffective, then medication may help reduce the *obsessionality* factor and enable you to better commit to your choices.

But for many people with OCD, life with medication isn't easy. It's not uncommon for people to try multiple medications (and combinations of medications) before they find one that really clicks with their brain chemistry. The medications that are effective for OCD are typically very slow acting and take several weeks or months at the therapeutic dose before demonstrating their effectiveness. And even then they may not demonstrate anything but side effects. It can be very frustrating. Some people take medication for short periods, some take them off and on, some take several medications throughout their lifetime, and some find one that clicks for them and remain on it indefinitely. Employing mindfulness and self-compassion tools can be instrumental in maintaining compliance and tolerance of medication; we will discuss how to do this in the next section.

Making Sense of Side Effects

What we refer to as "side effects" are best understood as "effects that are not the reason you took the medication." Every medication is designed to produce a wanted effect, but introducing a chemical to the body is not always the surgical strike we hope it will be, but creates other effects as well.

175

Wanted Effects

- Reduced depressive symptoms

- Reduced anxiety symptoms

- Reduced intensity of thought intrusion

- Increased ability to tolerate emotional and psychological discomforts

- Increased ability to resist compulsions and commit to CBT/ERP treatment

Unwanted Effects

- Increased anxiety or fatigue

- Emotional numbness

- Reduced libido

- Insomnia

- Headaches

- Stomach/digestive issues

- Nightmares/vivid dreams

- Various sensations (such as skin burning sensations, "brain zaps")

- Dry mouth

Common Obsessive Fears Related to Medication

What if I...

- Have a permanent psychosexual dysfunction?

- Lose my sense of identity on meds?

- Can't ever get off the meds?

- Forgot my dose or doubled my dose in error?

- Contaminated my pills?

- Develop a deadly side effect?

- Am not as courageous as people who don't take meds and am "cheating" by taking them?

If you have any of these common obsessive fears about medication, and your psychiatrist has already answered these what-if questions, but you've concluded that it's your OCD that isn't letting them go, it might benefit you to play an ERP game about this aspect of your treatment.

Using Mindfulness and Self-Compassion to Navigate Life with Meds

Self-compassion coping statements can be very useful for navigating life with meds, as they can help you remember how compassionate it is to give yourself access to all avenues of treatment. When you take a medication, you hand over a great deal of control to the prescribing doctor and to the pill or capsule itself. You make educated decisions under professional guidance, but the results are not always easy to predict. However, self-criticism when things are not going the way you want may be easier to predict. Let's look at the three elements of self-compassion (mindfulness, common humanity, and self-kindness) as they relate to life with medication.

Mindfulness

Remember, mindfulness is about being honest about your experience, without judgment and without getting carried away in storylines. For side effects in particular, mindfulness skills that emphasize sitting with, noting, and allowing physical sensations can be very helpful. If, for example, you have a side effect of dry mouth from medication, a mindfulness statement would be "My mouth is dry" and not "I hate these meds and nothing ever works for me!" In other words, dry mouth is a dryness of the mouth, and mindfulness is making space for experiencing that sensation as it is. Or if you are feeling discouraged by ongoing OCD symptoms while on medication, a mindful statement might be, "I'm frustrated that I am still having symptoms" as opposed to "My medication was a waste of time and money." You are observing the emotion, not criticizing its origin. It's not that the alternate or opposing statements are inherently false—they could be true—but to be mindful is to observe only what *is* and to not get distracted by what *could be*.

Common Humanity

In our clinical experience, the majority of people in treatment for OCD try some type of medication at some point in the process. It's easy to fall prey to the notion that taking medication is a sign of weakness. People feel the same way about addressing mental health in any capacity. But if you are advocating for your mental health, that is an act of bravery, whether you employ medication in your arsenal or not. Sadly, it's all too common for people with OCD to languish and wait for help that may never come. It takes courage to assert yourself enough to collect information on what tools (including this book) are available for getting better—but that's the only way you can find out which of them might help you. Medication is not for everyone, but it is one of the treatment tools available. So a good common humanity statement if you are feeling uncomfortable about taking medication for OCD might be, "Many people are wary of the idea of taking medication." Or if you are struggling with a side effect, you might acknowledge, "These sensations are common for people on this medication, and nobody enjoys this part of it." These statements of common humanity help you recognize that you are not alone; that many people experience the same struggles and fears about medications that you do.

Self-Kindness

Medication may make you feel better. It may make you feel worse. It may oscillate between the two and make you feel like you're on a mental-emotional roller coaster. Above all, it is important to give yourself permission to feel a loss of control when you take medication, because you aren't in control of how your body reacts to it. Since getting better from OCD is all about the bigger picture of letting go of control, taking medication can be a kind of exposure. Self-kindness is about opening yourself up to feeling out of control and not having all the answers each step along the way. Maybe this side effect will subside in a week or two. Maybe the side effect itself means the medication is going to be effective. Maybe the side effect is not there, but seems like it's there, but all the checking has you confused. These are all perfectly acceptable positions to find yourself in when interacting with medication.

So consider self-kindness statements like "I'm doing the best I can, and I'm going to invite myself to stay off of Google, and if I'm still feeling this way tomorrow, I'll call my psychiatrist." Giving yourself permission to just be with how you are feeling without having to do anything to "fix" it right now can create a tremendous feeling of relief. As with other aspects of your experience, remember that self-kindness is an invitation to acknowledge how well you're coping and point you in a helpful direction, the way you would treat a friend.

OCD's Unhappy Cousin: Depression

Did you know that it's *completely normal* for you to feel depressed at times if you have OCD? In fact, most people who have OCD also have its unhappy cousin, depression, or a lower-grade form of depression called *dysthymia*, at some point during their lives (Crino and Andrews 1996).

If you think about OCD, with its vicious cycle of intrusive, unwanted obsessions and exhausting, demoralizing compulsions, it makes logical sense that eventually, if you have OCD, you may also encounter depression.

If you do become depressed, you may start thinking things like, "Why am I depressed? This is so unfair. I have OCD and now I have depression, too. I need to figure out why I'm depressed and fix it, because I can't live like this!" Unfortunately, that way of thinking is likely to just make your depression worse. A more accepting, self-compassionate stance will be more likely to help you feel better, as we'll explain in the following tips for managing depression when you have OCD.

Using Self-Compassion in Response to Depression

In a recent article, the authors highlighted a number of studies showing that self-criticism predicts depression, relapse of depression, and poorer response to some types of treatment for depression (Warren, Smeets, and Neff 2016). Therefore, when you are starting to feel depressed, you'll want to use your self-compassion tools consistently. Here's an example:

"I'm feeling depressed right now. According to the book on OCD management I just read, a majority of people with OCD feel depressed at some point, so this is totally normal. I'm going to tell myself that it's okay that I'm feeling like this, recognizing that feeling depressed is just part of OCD recovery."

When you speak to yourself self-compassionately about depression, you are mindfully aware of how you are feeling, you normalize your feelings by recognizing they are common among people who suffer from OCD, and you give yourself permission to feel just as you do. Although giving yourself permission to feel depressed may sound like a way to become more depressed, it actually isn't. Instead, the acceptance tends to reduce rumination on the cyclical question of "But *why* am I depressed?" It's focusing on *that* question that can actually exacerbate depressed feelings (Segal, Teasdale, and Williams 2002).

Once you've spoken to yourself self-compassionately, choose a few of the other self-compassion exercises in part 2 of this book, especially activities that get you out of the house and interacting with people, and engage in one or two of them a day to help bolster your reserves of compassion toward yourself.

Do the Opposite, Just Like with OCD

Depression wants to control your behavior in much the same way OCD does. When you are depressed, you are driven away from certain behaviors and toward others. To stand up to depression you have to do the things you don't want to do, knowing that depression takes away the tools (motivation, self-esteem, self-compassion) that help you do those things. Doing the opposite is really hard. But just as you have done the opposite of what OCD wants so many times before, you can do the same with depression.

Here are some quick tips for doing the opposite of what depression wants:

- Depression wants you to isolate. Even though it may be difficult, reach out to people whose company you enjoy, and socialize.

183

- Depression wants you to shut down. Do the opposite, and start a new exercise routine or play some sports.

- Depression wants your environment to be depression-friendly. Make your environment incompatible with depression. Pull up the blinds and bring sunlight into your home. Play inspiring music, sing, dance, cook…

Ask for Help

Sometimes depression can come and go in a matter of days or even hours. Other times, it will hang around for a lot longer, and you need help to find the blue sky that's hidden by all the gray clouds. That help may vary, depending on where you are in your OCD recovery. If you have never sought treatment for OCD and you are feeling depressed, find a good CBT/ERP therapist to assist you in your recovery journey.

If you are in OCD treatment, tell your therapist about your depression, and she will make recommendations for how to treat it. In our experience, especially for people going through OCD treatment for the first time, many symptoms of depression may resolve as OCD symptoms recede through ERP.

If you've already been through OCD treatment and it seems your depression is not lifting, give your therapist a call for a booster session, so that she can assess whether your depression needs professional attention.

To sum up what to do to deal with the recurrence of depression when you have OCD: recognize that it's totally normal, be compassionate with yourself, identify whether you need help, and then reach out for the help you need, whether that's from a professional or through a self-help program if appropriate. It can be a delicate balance to be okay with depression being there and doing what you need to in order to compassionately and mindfully treat it; sometimes having a professional's guidance, even for a short time, can make all the difference. The goal is to learn to accept that depression may wash over you from time to time, and to know yourself well enough to understand when you need help to keep the depression from tossing you around in waves of despair and pulling you out to sea.

Other Forces That Impact OCD

A good way to stay on top of your OCD as it ebbs and flows is to make yourself knowledgeable about external and internal factors that may lead to a spike in symptoms. The list may actually be quite long (as is the journey), but knowing what typically precedes greater OCD challenges can give you the upper hand in staying on track. Let's take a look at three issues that can have a complex effect on your OCD.

Stress

In his book *Freedom from Obsessive-Compulsive Disorder* (2014), Dr. Jonathan Grayson explains why stress can be such a trigger for OCD. When you're in a really bad OCD episode, you feel all the hallmarks of stress. Therefore, feelings of stress become associated with OCD and can then be actual triggers of future OCD episodes. One study showed that perceived stress is significantly correlated with the intensity of obsessive symptoms (Morgado et al. 2013). In other words, the more stress you have, the louder your intrusive thoughts are likely to be. It's worth noting that even stressors that are considered positive (getting married, starting a new job, buying a home, and so on) can still exacerbate your OCD.

In stressful situations, it's best to be mindfully aware that OCD is probably lurking around the corner somewhere, and then to pull out a few preemptive ERP games to proactively deal with it. Or, if a stressful situation pops up out of nowhere, just remember that intrusive thoughts are likely to also arise during this time. This can make their appearance less surprising and easier to address.

Finally, as Kelly McGonigal says in her TED Talk, "How to Make Stress Your Friend" (2013), our perception of stress, as well our willingness to reach out to others for support and encouragement, can make a huge difference in how stress affects us: "How you think and how you act can transform your experience of stress. When you choose to view your stress response as helpful, you create the biology of courage. And when you choose to connect with others under stress, you can create resilience…when you choose to view stress in this way, you're not just getting better at stress, you're actually making a pretty profound statement. You're saying that you can trust yourself to handle life's challenges. And you're remembering that you don't have to face them alone."

An OCD episode is a huge stressor in and of itself. Dr. McGonigal's recommendations about interpreting stress as positive are analogous to ours in chapter 4 about approaching OCD with an attitude of J-O-Y, as this shifts your perspective from one of fear to one of empowerment. Her findings also echo the importance we place on reaching out to others so that you'll know you are not alone in dealing with OCD.

Sleep

A recent review of research on sleep and OCD found that it's pretty common for people with OCD to have some type of sleep disturbance, which may include shorter sleep duration, lower sleep efficiency (the ratio of total time asleep to the total time spent in bed during a night), perceived lower sleep quality, and having trouble going to sleep. While there are some theories as to why people with OCD experience disturbed sleep, at this point no one really understands why this occurs (Paterson et al. 2013).

Needless to say, good sleep is important if you have OCD, but paradoxically, it may be hard to get! Just as when we discussed depression, we aren't sharing this information to bring you down or to make you worry about sleep—far from it! Instead, we want to help normalize the potentially disturbed experience of sleep (or lack thereof) in people with OCD. It's one of those things that we want to self-compassionately acknowledge: "It makes sense that sometimes I sleep poorly, as that happens to people with OCD." You also want to recognize that if you've had a night (or several nights) of poor sleep, you may have more trouble with OCD bothering you, and continue your self-compassion statement with: "and that's okay. I'm going to do what I can to manage my OCD today, knowing it may be more active, and I may give in to a slip or two because I'm sort of tired." This is a good example of owning your OCD and being honest about the experience of life with the disorder, which helps you to both self-compassionately accept the situation and feel empowered to fight doing compulsions to the best of your ability.

Substance Abuse

Though some people find their OCD makes them so threat-averse that they actively avoid any recreational drugs (and sometimes avoid prescribed and needed drugs as well), a statistically relevant number of OCD sufferers also struggle with substance abuse (Blom et al. 2011).

People with OCD and addiction face a hard path; there's no denying this. Many have found some temporary relief from the cacophony of their minds by checking out and immersing themselves in alcohol or drugs. When their lives become unmanageable as a result, they face the same challenge as any addict to learn to live a healthy and meaningful sober life. But once the addiction is behind them, the OCD is right there waiting, taunting, nudging them back toward addiction.

Furthermore, a person with OCD may find himself being compulsive about sobriety, constantly checking and analyzing to get certainty that he has not slipped and accidentally relapsed and that he is not somehow being dishonest about his clean date (the date he began sobriety). It is not hard to imagine the challenge of having something called a *clean date* and also navigating recovery from OCD. But people do accomplish both, and more and more attention is being given to helping people suffering from dual diagnoses achieve a dual recovery.

It would be impractical to cover the pros and cons of every recreational drug in this book, so in terms of determining what works for you, consider the following questions:

- Do I have a history of problematic use of this substance or anything similar?

- What is my primary intention here? Enjoyment or escape?

- Is this a direct response to an intrusive thought and an attempt to compulsively avoid?

- Can I achieve the results I am seeking in some other way?

- Do the people who know and support me know about and support this behavior?

The point is not that you have to be perfect. Cultural practices, family medical history, and a host of other factors contribute to a person's decision to engage with or abstain from mind-altering "recreational" substances. We recommend simply being mindful of (and honest with yourself about) the role substance use may play in navigating life with OCD. If it is causing more problems than it is alleviating, then a self-compassionate approach may be trying your best to keep use of substances to a minimum.

Your Everyday Takeaway

Understanding your long-term trajectory with OCD means having insight into the things that precipitate and aggravate your OCD symptoms. This holds true whether you feel you're in a bad state with the OCD or you feel you are doing well. Mastery is found in eliminating OCD's ability to surprise you. No one knows the types of thoughts, and the type of thinking, that gets you trapped in an obsessive-compulsive loop the way you do. If you get surprised and start interacting with an intrusive thought like it's new and unique information, you may endure a lot of suffering as you struggle to access your mindfulness and CBT/ERP tools. This leads to shame and self-criticism, and you can lose sight of self-compassion.

If, instead, you develop the capacity to view your unwanted thoughts as typical, unimpressive, and predictable, you can respond gracefully with mindfulness, exposure, or a simple roll of your eyes. Above all, learning to love yourself while observing what *is*, instead of judging yourself for sometimes getting lost in what *could be*, makes the difference between living painfully and living joyfully with OCD.

In this book, we have taken a somewhat different approach to OCD self-help than you might find in many of the excellent CBT/ERP self-treatment guides. Our focus has been less on teaching you what OCD is and creating a treatment plan from scratch and more on connecting the concepts of mindfulness and self-compassion to the journey you are already on. This is a book about long-term mastery over OCD, and as such, we chose to speak to you as the OCD veteran you are instead of an OCD rookie.

So what do we hope you have learned? First, we hope you now know that mindfulness is not some weird new age concept that's meant to exclude people with OCD. To the contrary, mindfulness is for thinkers, and OCD sufferers are big thinkers. Learning to view your thoughts, feelings, and sensations without judgment can help you capitalize on your unique skill of noticing what others may overlook, while also reducing your attachment to suffering.

We also hope you have learned that the cruel, critical OCD voice in your head is not your own voice, but just a stream of thought that you can challenge and mold toward self-compassion. Using self-compassion skills can lead you to view your OCD experience more honestly and openly, recognizing that you are not alone in the universe as a person with sometimes scary thoughts and feelings, and choosing behaviors that are grounded in kindness and helpfulness instead of submission to your disorder.

We encourage you to experiment with the mindfulness and self-compassion exercises, as well as the ERP games, and create your own repertoire for being in command of your OCD. In the end, we hope you will learn to love yourself with OCD, whether you are mostly symptom free or face-to-face with your symptoms in this moment. After all, you are your own best companion, and you're actually pretty amazing.

References

Abramowitz, Jonathan S., Brett J. Deacon, and Stephen P. H. Whiteside. 2011. *Exposure Therapy for Anxiety: Principles and Practice*. New York: The Guilford Press.

American Psychiatric Association. 2013. *Diagnostic and Statistical Manual of Mental Disorders*, 5th edition. Washington, DC.

Baer, Lee. 2002. *The Imp of the Mind: Exploring the Silent Epidemic of Obsessive Bad Thoughts*. New York: Plume.

Bell, Jeff. 2009. *When in Doubt, Make Belief: An OCD-Inspired Approach to Living with Uncertainty*. Novato, CA: New World Library.

Blom, Rianne M., Maarten Koeter, Wim van den Brink, Ron de Graaf, Margreet ten Have, and Damiaan Denys. 2011 "Co-occurrence of Obsessive-Compulsive Disorder and Substance Use Disorder in the General Population." *Addiction* 106, no. 12: 2178–2185.

Brown, Brené. 2010. *The Gifts of Imperfection: Let Go of Who You Think You're Supposed to Be and Embrace Who You Are*. Center City, MN: Hazelden.

Brown, Brené. 2013. *Brené Brown on Empathy*. Royal Society for the encouragement of Arts, Manufactures and Commerce. https://www.thersa.org/discover/videos/rsa-shorts/2013/12/Brene-Brown-on-Empathy.

Chodron, Pema. 2003. *Comfortable with Uncertainty: 108 Teachings on Cultivating Fearlessness and Compassion*, Nook edition. Boston: Shambhala Publications.

Craske, M. G., K. Kircanski, M. Zelikowsky, J. Mystkowski, N. Chowdhury, and A. Baker. 2008. "Optimizing Inhibitory Learning During Exposure Therapy." *Behaviour Research & Therapy* 46, no. 1: 5–27.

Craske, M. G., M. Treanor, C. C. Conway, T. Zbozinek, and B. Vervliet. 2014. "Maximizing Exposure Therapy: An Inhibitory Learning Approach." *Behaviour Research & Therapy* 58: 10–23.

Crino, R. D., and G. Andrews. 1996. "Obsessive-Compulsive Disorder and Axis I Comorbidity." *Journal of Anxiety Disorders* 10, no. 1: 37–46.

Cuddy, Amy. 2015. *Presence: Bringing Your Boldest Self to Your Biggest Challenges.* New York: Little, Brown and Company.

Davidson, Joan. 2014. *Daring to Challenge OCD: Overcome Your Fear of Treatment and Take Control of Your Life Using Exposure and Response Prevention.* Oakland, CA: New Harbinger Publications.

Germer, Christopher K. 2009. *The Mindful Path to Self-Compassion: Freeing Yourself from Destructive Thoughts and Emotions*, Nook edition. New York: The Guilford Press.

Goldstein, Elisha. 2012. *The Now Effect: How a Mindful Moment Can Change the Rest of Your Life.* New York: Atria Books.

Goldstein, Joseph. 2013. *Mindfulness: A Practical Guide to Awakening.* Boulder, CO: Sounds True.

Goldstein, J., and D. Harris. 2016. Day 1, *10% Happier*, "Am I a Failed Meditator?" In the course *More Than a Hobby*, accessed November 3, 2016. http://www.10percenthappier.com/

Goncalves, O. F., S. Carvalho, J. Leite, A. Fernandes-Goncalves, A. Carracedo, and A. Sampaio. 2016. "Cognitive and Emotional Impairments in Obsessive-Compulsive Disorder: Evidence from Functional Brain Alterations." *Porto Biomedical Journal* 1, no. 3: 92–105.

Grayson, J. B. 2010. "OCD and Intolerance of Uncertainty: Treatment Issues." *Journal of Cognitive Psychotherapy* 24, no. 1: 3–15.

Grayson, Jonathan. 2014. *Freedom from Obsessive Compulsive Disorder: A Personalized Recovery Program for Living with Uncertainty*, updated edition. New York: The Penguin Group.

Hershfield, Jon. 2015. *When a Family Member Has OCD: Mindfulness and Cognitive Behavioral Skills to Help Families Affected By Obsessive-Compulsive Disorder*. Oakland, CA: New Harbinger Publications.

Hershfield, Jon, and Tom Corboy. 2013. *The Mindfulness Workbook for OCD: A Guide to Overcoming Obsessions and Compulsions Using Mindfulness and Cognitive Behavioral Therapy*. Oakland, CA: New Harbinger Publications.

Dalai Lama, Desmond Tutu, and Douglas C. Abrams. 2016. *The Book of Joy: Lasting Happiness in a Changing World*. New York: Penguin Publishing Group.

McGonigal, Kelly. 2013. *How to Make Stress Your Friend*. TEDGlobal 2013.

McGrath, Patrick B. 2006. *Don't Try Harder, Try Different: A Workbook for Managing Anxiety and Stress*.

Morgado, P., D. Freitas, J. M. Bessa, N. Sousa, and João José Cerqueira. 2013. "Perceived Stress in Obsessive–Compulsive Disorder is Related with Obsessive but Not Compulsive Symptoms." *Frontiers in Psychiatry* 4: 21. doi:10.3389/fpsyt.2013.00021.

Murray, Christopher J. L., and Alan D. Lopez. 1996. *The Global Burden of Disease*. Cambridge, MA: Harvard University Press.

Neff, Kristin. 2011. *Self-Compassion: Stop Beating Yourself Up and Leave Insecurity Behind*. New York: William Morrow.

Paterson, J., A. C. Reynolds, S. A. Ferguson, and D. Dawson. 2013. "Sleep and Obsessive-Compulsive Disorder (OCD)." *Sleep Medicine Reviews* 17, no. 6: 465–474.

Pittman, Catherine M, and Elizabeth M. Karle. 2015. *Rewire Your Anxious Brain: How to Use the Neuroscience of Fear to End Anxiety, Panic, and Worry.* Oakland, CA: New Harbinger Publications.

Ralph, Stuart, and Jonathan Grayson. 2016. *The OCD Stories*, episode 45.

Renshaw, K. D., G. Steketee, and D. L. Chambless. "Involving Family Members in the Treatment of OCD." *Cognitive Behavior Therapy* 34 (2005): 164–175.

Sapolsky, Robert M. 2004. *Why Zebras Don't Get Ulcers*, 3rd edition. New York: Henry Holt and Company.

Segal, Zindel V., John D. Teasdale, and J. Mark G. Williams. 2002. *Mindfulness-Based Cognitive Therapy for Depression: A New Approach to Preventing Relapse*, 1st edition. New York: The Guilford Press.

Steketee, G. 1993. "Social Support and Treatment Outcome of Obsessive Compulsive Disorder at 9-Month Follow-up." *Behavioural and Cognitive Psychotherapy* 21, no. 2: 81–95.

Steketee, G., and B. Van Noppen. 2003. "Family Approaches to Treatment for Obsessive Compulsive Disorder." *Revista Brasileira de Psiquiatria* 25, no. 1: 43–50, https://dx.doi.org/10.1590/S1516–44462003000100009.

Warren, R., E. Smeets, and K. Neff. In press 2016. "Self-Criticism and Self-Compassion: Risk and Resilience for Psychopathology." *Current Psychiatry.*

Wilson, Reid. 2016. *Stopping the Noise in Your Head.* Deerfield Beach, FL: Health Communications, Inc.

Wiseman, T. 1996. "A Concept Analysis of Empathy." *Journal of Advanced Nursing* 23, no. 6: 1162–1167.

Jon Hershfield, MFT, is director of The OCD and Anxiety Center of Greater Baltimore in Hunt Valley, MD. He specializes in the mindfulness-based and cognitive behavioral treatment of obsessive-compulsive disorder (OCD), and is licensed in the states of Maryland, Virginia, and California. Hershfield is coauthor of *The Mindfulness Workbook for OCD*, and author of *When a Family Member Has OCD*. He is a frequent presenter at the annual conferences of both the International OCD Foundation and the Anxiety and Depression Association of America, and a professional contributor to multiple online OCD-related support groups and blogs.

Shala Nicely, LPC, is a cognitive behavioral therapy (CBT) therapist in metro Atlanta, GA, specializing in the treatment of OCD and related disorders. She was the keynote speaker for the 2013 International OCD Foundation (IOCDF) conference with the story of her triumph over OCD, "Is Fred in the Refrigerator?" Shala promotes the power of turning personal challenges into service to others as an advocate for The Adversity 2 Advocacy Alliance. She is cofounder, with Jeff Bell, of beyondthedoubt.com, an initiative dedicated to helping people learn to thrive through uncertainty and the fear and doubt it creates. Shala also blogs for *Psychology Today*, offering an inside perspective on life with OCD and the lessons of uncertainty.

Foreword writer **C. Alec Pollard, PhD**, is director of the Center for OCD and Anxiety-Related Disorders (COARD), and professor of family and community medicine at Saint Louis University School of Medicine. Pollard is a licensed psychologist who works with a range of obsessive-compulsive and anxiety-related disorders, with a special interest in patients ambivalent about or resistant to therapy. He serves as a reviewer for a number of professional journals and conference program committees, and has authored and coauthored more than eighty-five publications, including two books: *The Agoraphobia Workbook* and *Dying of Embarrassment*.

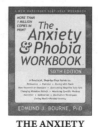

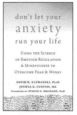